GREAT SOUL

BOOKS BY HERRYMON MAURER

GREAT SOUL · THE OLD FELLOW
THE END IS NOT YET

DOUBLEDAY & COMPANY, INC.

HERRYMON MAURER

GREAT SOUL

THE GROWTH OF GANDHI

GARDEN CITY, N. Y., 1949

CONTENTS

but violence appeared.
Gandhi halted the struggle.
The British put him in jail.   **55**

7. After he had come out of jail,
   Gandhi struggled to heal India's own ills,
   abandoning politics and
   traveling everywhere over the land.   60

8. Gandhi knew that Truth is in all men,
   making them one.
   During the years of traveling
   he taught three things:
   Truth, non-violence, simplicity.   73

9. A second great struggle against the British
   lasted three years and ended with Gandhi
   in jail, where he fasted
   on behalf of the untouchables.   83

10. During a second period of pause,
    Gandhi went on with his teaching.
    East and West looked at him,
    followed him, and yet misunderstood him.   89

11. From his simple community of Truth
    and non-violence he looked at a world of war.
    He led a third struggle against the British,
    again was put in jail.   102

12. India became free. But the country freed
    by a man of non-violence fell into violence,
    and the man of the power of Truth
    died from the power of a bullet.   114

    Comment.   124

GREAT SOUL

FOR ANN

1

*The greatness of Mahatma Gandhi
was not simply that he freed India,
but that he himself grew toward Truth.*

Into a world lighted by Truth, fed by it, kept alive by it, but yet ignorant of it, there came a man who sought it, felt it, and declared it. Truth is of God, and it is God. It is that which all men see in part without any seeing fully, which all seek without any knowing fully why they seek it. It is that which men forget until it grows within one of themselves.

This man, whom people called Mahatma, the Great Soul, lived so that men could know that there is a power more real than the power of money or weapons or prisons, and that through it men could break the ancient chains of violence, which enslave in darkness and death the children and the children's children of those whose involvement in evil is greater than their love of good.

Many men saw Gandhi, but the world, made up of men, did not see. For the world struck him with blows, betrayed him with bloodshed, and killed him. Yet in a world of oppression and killings Gandhi lived Truth; in a world of frivolities he sought Truth; in a world where the strong hurt the weak he fought back with Truth; in a world where men boasted their goodness

9

he hid himself in Truth; in a world where men were in bondage he found freedom in Truth. For his aim was not alone to cease war, live simply, raise up the weak, and take upon himself the evil of others. His aim was that men might, like him, grow in Truth.

He put himself last; hence he found himself first. He wished to be humble; hence he became great. He had the strength of water, which, as it seeks a low place, wears away rock and soil, and nothing can stop it. When Gandhi spoke, people crowded around him in numbers beyond counting, and millions of them willingly did as he asked, even though he asked them to be jailed, beaten, or made poor. The poor in goods and the poor in spirit looked into his face and, seeing the light by which he understood them, understood him. He so put his touch upon the people of India and the people of Britain that India became free. Upon men given to violence he put the way of *Satyagraha*— the power of Truth in which there is no violence. Upon men so given to caste that they would not even let the shadow of men of the lower order fall upon them, he put the conviction that untouchables are brothers. For Gandhi so loved Truth that others, loving him, loved it.

Whatever kept him off from Truth he cast out, and whatever yoked him closer to it he hung onto. He did not reason the way of God but experienced it, hearing Him as sharply as the noise of thunder or the quiet of night. The great wonder of his life was not the freeing of India or the healing of some of her ills, but the silence wherein he prayed and listened. By this experience made fearless of death, hunger, or imprisonment, he abandoned as obstacles all the ways of the world—the world's violence, the world's lies, its vanities, its greed. It was by first seeking Truth that he found the power by which the slavery and violence of the world are overcome.

2

His soul was not always great.
When young he fell into perplexity
and shame, and he was kept alive
only by a hidden sense of Truth.

The outward form in which inward Truth developed was insignificant. Mahatma Gandhi was a short, thin little man with a dark skin, a scrawny form, great ears, and deep, clear eyes. He dressed as poorly as the lowest of his people, and he lived either in jails or in huts made from the earth on which they were set. His physical strength was trivial; his intellect was not exceptional; and his words were neither sparkling nor magical. Other men have written weightier books, had more subtle thoughts, made more impassioned speeches, practiced more remarkable meditations, given greater sermons. Gandhi said:

"I have not the qualifications for teaching my philosophy of life. I have barely qualifications for practicing the philosophy I believe. I am but a poor, struggling soul yearning to be wholly good—wholly truthful and wholly non-violent in thought, word, and deed, but ever failing to reach the ideal which I know to be true."

In one thing was Mahatma Gandhi great above all else, in that he knew the presence of Truth as sharply as if it were something he could touch and see and hear, falling back in all things upon that presence with a courage so complete that it ceased to be courage and became love.

The great fact of his life was growth. He never ceased growing, and in his earlier years he had to grow greatly. For his soul was not always great, and when he was young he was much troubled, suffering temptations of lust, comfort, and outward strength, even as saints in other times and places, men such as Gautama or Saint Francis, have suffered them. Married without choice at the age of thirteen in a country where women were secluded and matters of sex kept hidden, he was thrown into great perplexity and great feelings of shame. He was unable to keep up with his schoolwork, and fell into irritability, even suffering suspicion of his wife Kasturbai. He was pressed down by fears of thieves, ghosts, and serpents, and he confessed, "I did not dare to stir out of the house at night. Darkness was a terror to me."

He was born in the city of Porbandar in the year 1869, a time when the ancient rules of rank and family were weighty and when duty insisted that a man give merit to caste and clan. The Hindu religion had long given stress to the duties of each man in his particular calling in life, and during the course of time it had built up rigid classes composed of persons of like callings. What is more, this religion had the belief that the progress of a man's spirit was not confined to one life on this earth, but that progress could go on through various lives. This belief became

13

falsely tied up with the system of castes—higher, lower, and outcaste—so that a man of inferior status was considered a man of inferior spirit, and a man of higher status was obliged to follow complicated rules of behavior in order to show that his caste was one of better rebirth. Consequently, the people of India were sharply acute to the honor of the group into which they were born, in particular such of the people as belonged to the topmost classes. Mohandas Karamchand Gandhi came into a family that was high placed, his father and his father's fathers having served as prime ministers of certain small principalities of India. The family was strict in the forms of the Hindu religion; and upon young Gandhi fell obligations to family and duties to uphold honor that it took many years to overcome. In his youth he underwent great fears of insult or reprimand. Whipped once, he wept piteously. He was forever seeking some trick of becoming strong like the Britons who ruled his country, and he was forever suffering shame at his weakness.

This hankering after outward strength took him into a period of temptation, during which he became the close friend of a person whom his mother, his brother, and his wife warned him against—a young man who could run long distances and jump great heights. This friend laid his hardiness to the eating of meat—a thing forbidden by the Hindu religion, which treats all life, not simply human life, as sacred—and avoided as sin by Gandhi's family. Eager for physical

14

prowess and blindly devoted to his friend, Gandhi went out to a lonely place beside a river and took some bits of goat's flesh. Then he became sick, and at night he dreamed of a goat bleating within him, but he clung to his friendship and went to restaurants until his distaste for meat left him.

But it was the aim of this friend not only to upset Gandhi on matters of food but on matters of sex as well. For he planted in Gandhi's mind untrue suspicions of the faithfulness of his young wife, and persuaded him to go to a brothel. The false friend had planned all beforehand, even the payment, but when Gandhi came into the place, he was almost struck blind and dumb, and he fled. This experience happened other times, and each time Gandhi felt an agony of shame.

Fearful he was; cowardly he was; for he was incomplete. But he was held up by a dimly sensed need for Truth, albeit in its smaller forms. To eat meat he had to deceive his parents, who could not have borne the knowledge of his eating it, and his lies tormented him so that he gave up meat altogether, not because he then thought it evil, but because he would no longer take leave of Truth.

But the time for an end of his torments was not at hand. He stole the pocket money of servants to buy cigarettes, which he smoked in secret because of the stern beliefs of his family. He wanted to have both one thing and the opposite of that thing. Thus he looked upon adults with great awe and had an urge

15

to be greatly filial, but he also had a great urge to be his own man and do what he wanted. He had also a particular urge to the activity of sex. And all these urges conflicted within him. One night, as his father lay dying, he gave over rubbing his father's weakened body to come together with his wife, who was presently expecting a child. While they were together, his father died. A little later the child was born dead. That night tortured him for a long time with shame.

Yet Truth never left him. He resolved to kill himself because he could not do as he wished, and to that end he went out into the forests to gather poison nuts. But when he had come into an obscure corner of a temple and swallowed one or two of the nuts, he knew in himself that he did not wish to die. Again, he once stole a piece of gold from his brother to settle a debt, and Truth moved in him so strongly that, although he was too shamed to speak out, he wrote down what he had done and went to his father.

"I was trembling all over," he wrote later, "as I handed the confession to my father. He was then suffering from fistula and was confined to bed. His bed was a bare plank of wood. I handed him the note and sat opposite. As he read it through, tears like pearl drops trickled down his cheeks, wetting the paper. For a moment he closed his eyes in thought and then tore up the note. He had sat up to read it. He again lay down. I also shed tears when I saw my father's agony. . . . Those pearl drops of love cleansed my heart and washed my sin away. Only he who has experienced such love can know what it is. As the hymn says:

> *Only he*
> *Who is smitten with the arrows of love*
> *Knows its power.*

One thing took root in him, that Truth is the stuff of goodness.

But although he had come to sense Truth, he did not yet see it as God, and not seeing it did not understand its power. For many years he was to know shame, bear uncertainty, and even make display. He was sent to London to study law, and on his arrival in England, seeing that he alone wore white clothes, he felt shame sweep again over him. To make outward display, he undertook to learn Western dancing, bought a silk hat and a dress suit, and started violin and elocution lessons. After a time he gave over the lessons, but he tried for some years to be foppish in dress.

When he came home to India, he brought British methods of living into his household, and the expense of the house increased. He could not get clients for his law practice, and he went away to the large city of Bombay, but his failure there was great. He had but one case in court, and he became tongue-tied so that he could not speak. Thereupon he went back to his home again, where he found some small work in writing up memorials and applications.

At this time, too, a new sense of shame settled upon him. It so happened that the local British

17

political agent had become prejudiced against Gandhi's brother. This man had been friendly to Gandhi in England, and Gandhi went to him to plead.

The political agent became stiff, and he said, "Your brother is an intriguer. I want to hear nothing more from you. I have no time. If your brother has anything to say, let him apply through the proper channel."

And when Gandhi attempted to speak, the political agent said, "You must go now."

Then Gandhi replied, "But please hear me out." But the political agent called his servant and had Gandhi put out of the room.

This insult meant not only shame but insecurity. Gandhi considered that not only his honor had been brooked but that his work had been jeopardized, for his law practice could not long continue in a place where a hostile man was the final authority of government.

It was at this time that there came to him an offer to leave home for South Africa and work there at law for a firm of Indian merchants. Gandhi went away quickly. He went away uncertain, unsettled, still incomplete, and troubled with a new consciousness of the shame of belonging to a colored and conquered race.

3

As a lawyer in South Africa,
Gandhi could have won great wealth,
but he eschewed it to serve
the oppressed and to fight evil
with the power of Truth.

In India there was the disdain of foreign rulers for the natives they ordered about. In South Africa there was the prejudice of a people of one color living in the midst of a people of another color, and Gandhi had fresh experience of shame. He came into the city of Durban in the province of Natal, where Indians were called coolies or sammies, and after a few days he visited the courts, from which he was thrown out because he would not take off his turban. Shortly thereafter he was sent out to work in a neighboring area, the Transvaal, and he was ordered out of a train because he was a colored man traveling first-class.

Gandhi said, "I was permitted to travel in this compartment at Durban, and I insist on going on in it."

The railway official said, "No, you won't. You must leave this compartment, or else I shall have to call a police constable to push you out."

But Gandhi remained firm, and he said, "Yes, you may. I refuse to get out voluntarily."

Gandhi was forced from the train, and his baggage was taken from it. He went to the waiting room, where he took thought as to what he should do. The night was cold, and Gandhi's overcoat was in his baggage, but he feared to ask for it lest he be insulted again. He considered whether he should throw up his work and go back to India. But it came to his mind that the insult that had been done him was only a thing of the surface, and that underneath there lay the deep disease of prejudice against color; and he decided that he should not only go on with his work but make himself ready to suffer hardship so that the disease itself might be rooted out.

Gandhi had been put off the train in the town of Maritzburg, and in the morning the Indian merchants of that place came to console him, but they could console him only with stories of their own hardships. In the evening Gandhi took the train again and went on without trouble. But he had to travel a distance by stagecoach, and the conductor of the coach would not let him sit inside. After a time he would not even let him sit any longer on the coach box outside. The conductor pointed to the dirty footboard of the coach and said:

"Sammy, you sit on this; I want to sit near the driver."

Gandhi trembled with shame and with fear, but he would not come down from the box. The man swore and used great strength trying to pull Gandhi down,

20

but Gandhi clung to the brass rails of the box and would not let go. Then the people inside the coach cried out against the conductor and insisted that Gandhi be seated inside among them.

When Gandhi finally reached the Transvaal he was the same Gandhi but yet a new Gandhi, for the idea of serving others had come into his mind. Shortly after his arrival he called a meeting of Indians of all faiths—Hindus, Mussalmans (Moslems), Parsis, and Christians—to discuss ways by which they could better their lot. He had then seen more closely into the condition of his countrymen, and he was moved by their hardships. They had been brought into South Africa by Europeans under a system of indenture, whereby they slaved five years at the plantations and mines and then became free. But the Europeans objected to free Indians and levied taxes and passed laws against them. In their newspapers they said, "These Indians have no sense of human decency. They suffer from loathsome diseases. They consider every woman as their prey." (Gandhi once observed that "the human intellect delights in inventing specious arguments in order to support injustice.") Stirred, he spoke in public for the first time, and his words also stirred those who heard him, for thereafter Indians sought him out.

In the Transvaal the work of Gandhi was to aid the lawsuit of one Indian Mussalman against another, both being well-to-do traders. But he was troubled that one person should attempt to destroy the well-being of another. He was certain that his own client could win at court, but he convinced both parties to seek arbitration. When his client was awarded a large claim in money, he sought means whereby the opponent could repay the sum without being ruined. This attachment to goodness brought him new respect from the community.

Meanwhile, encouraged by European Christians and Indian Mussalmans, he gave himself over to study and thought, reading the scriptures of Christianity, Muhammadanism, and of his own old great but decaying Hindu religion, poring over the Bible, over Tolstoy and Thoreau, examining the *Light of the East* and the *Gita*. His mind began to ease. But the first fruit of his growth in Truth was not a preaching of ideas but more work for his people. It was in this work that he taught himself to listen to the inner voice, and it was in this work, he said, that ". . . the religious spirit within me became a living force. . . ."

It had been settled that he would go back to India at the end of one year, and he left the Transvaal for Natal to take passage from the city of Durban. But a bill had been introduced in that area to take the vote away from Indians, and when his countrymen in Natal pressed him to remain, Gandhi agreed to stay for a month. He drew up petitions, held meetings, and secured ten thousand signatures on a memorial to the government. And again he made ready to leave South Africa.

But Indians came to him and said, "You yourself have explained to us that this is the first step taken with a view to our ultimate extinction. . . . You have now witnessed our enthusiasm. We are willing to work and we have funds. But for want of a guide, what little has been already done will go to nothing. We therefore regard it to be your duty to stay on."

Seeing thus the course of service, Gandhi refused to take any salary and made ready to support himself through the practice of law. Thereupon in May 1894 he formed the Natal Indian Congress, a group which was to struggle for the rights of the Indian settlers. One year had passed since he arrived in South Africa, and many new ideas kept coming into his mind: education of the young, action to overcome the shortcomings of Indians, not simply those of Europeans, and co-operation with all races and peoples, whenever possible on a footing of equality.

He had not only fresh ideas on politics but fresh ideas on law. He would not take a case if his client would not speak the truth. Once, when a man brought suit but indicated by his answering in court that he was not truthful, Gandhi moved that his client's suit be dismissed. His client begged him for forgiveness; other men came begging him for his services.

Once his friend Parsi Rustomji, an importer of goods, came to him to confess that he had been caught smuggling, albeit in an offense involving only a small sum of money. The Parsi begged Gandhi to save him.

But Gandhi said, "To save or not to save you is in His hands. As for me, you know my way: I can but try to save you by means of a confession."

The name and wealth and freedom of this man were at stake, but he said, "Well, I have told you that I am entirely in your hands. You may do just as you like."

Gandhi took the Parsi's confession for all the smuggling he had done, not just the smuggling at which he had been caught, and he took it to the court, there to plead for his friend. The court was moved; a fine instead of a jail sentence was imposed; and Parsi Rustomji framed the confession and put it on the wall of his office by way of a warning to other merchants.

In such ways Gandhi sought to grow in the practice of Truth, but his Truth was more than mere honesty, for it included love and forgiveness, and the use of these in his own life began to free him from the fear of insult and shame. One day, when he had been in South Africa only a short time, a sentry threw him into the street in front of the house of the President of the Transvaal because his skin was dark. A European friend came running to him, saying, "Gandhi, I have seen everything. I shall gladly be your witness in court if you proceed against the man. I am very sorry you have been so rudely assaulted."

But Gandhi said, "You need not be sorry. What does the poor man know? All colored people are the same to him. He no doubt treats Negroes just as he has treated me. I have made it a rule not to go to court in respect of any personal grievance. So I do not intend to proceed against him."

Then the sentry apologized, but Gandhi said there was no need, since he had already forgiven him.

In 1897, when Gandhi was more grievously attacked, he was equally forgiving. He had gone home the year before to bring his family to South Africa, and while in India he had written a pamphlet about Natal. A Reuters newspaperman cabled a false account of the pamphlet, and the Europeans of Natal gave way to feelings of anger and outrage. On his return Gandhi landed at Durban and started walking toward the house of Parsi Rustomji, where he and his family were to stay. At once the cry went up, "Here's Gandhi, here's Gandhi! Thrash him! Surround him!" A mob gathered and it began to curse and throw stones. One man slapped and kicked Gandhi so hard that consciousness almost left him. But he determined to walk on, warding off no blows, even if it cost him his life. At last he reached Rustomji's house only because the wife of the superintendent of police, who was passing by, came to walk beside him. Thus he was spared critical injuries. Finally the mob surrounded Rustomji's house and shouted that they would burn it unless Gandhi was delivered over to them. But the police superintendent spirited Gandhi out of the house and into a place of safety.

The press of Natal had already talked with Gandhi before he left the boat, and learning of the falseness of the report from Reuters, they wrote sympathetically. The mood of the city of Durban changed altogether, and the attorney general came to Gandhi to ask him to identify those who had attacked him, that

they might be arrested and tried. But Gandhi would
neither identify anyone nor have anyone prosecuted,
explaining that he did not hold the mob at fault. He
said, "Prosecuting my assailants is therefore out of
the question. This is a religious question with me."

He would not only forgive his opponents; he would
seek ways of helping them. In the year 1899 the war
between the British and the Boers broke out, and
Gandhi convinced other Indians that they should act
loyally toward the Empire even if the Empire did not
always act justly toward them. (He then believed that
the British system was for the good of mankind.)
Therefore he set up a group of stretcher bearers and
worked with them under fire. Some years later he
led another corps when a rebellion appeared among
the African Zulu people. He found comfort that
these works aided both sides of the conflict, but he
believed their great value lay in the taking on of
tasks of citizenship, the privileges of which were many
times denied to Indians.

All this while he grew in simplicity of outward
living. The compelling power of his own being had
become evident, and the way opened to him for success in the practice of law. Clients came to him in
great numbers, and he looked to be a worldly success,
a respected citizen who was beginning to make a
fortune. But the more money came in, the more
money he tried to give out. He furnished his house
with only the most necessary furniture; he took over
grinding meal and baking his own bread; he even

started washing his shirts. On a visit to India in 1902 he began traveling third-class in railways and steamships. Possessions and extravagances he had come to understand as encumbrances upon him.

While he made his living simpler, he enlarged his household. To his family, made up of his wife Kasturbai and their four sons, he added more family— friends of all beliefs, for among the Indians there were Hindus and Mussalmans, and among the Europeans there were Christians and Jews. At the marriage of a Jewish-Christian couple, his friends the Polaks, he served as best man, and they came to live within his household. ". . . I have known no distinction," he wrote, "between relatives and strangers, countrymen and foreigners, white and colored, Hindus and Indians of other faiths, whether Mussalmans, Parsis, Christians, or Jews. I may say that my heart has been incapable of making any such distinction. I cannot claim this as a special virtue, as it has been in my very nature, rather than a result of any effort on my part. . . ." His heart was never touched by the petty differences of religions, and he knew no difference of race. He even became angry with Kasturbai—and anger was rare with him even then—when she found it hard to bring herself to empty the slops of a young man born to parents of the caste that Hindus believed untouchable.

In the year 1904 his inward growth reached its first great climax. He was then living in Johannesburg in the Transvaal, where he had been called two years earlier to aid the plight of Indians in that province, which by then forbade their re-entry into the place once they had left it. It happened that black plague developed in one of the mining camps and spread to twenty-three of the Indians working in the mine, and Gandhi undertook to stop the epidemic and to nurse the sick through the course of their fatal and often contagious disease. He asked his four law clerks to come help, and they followed him. He summoned a European physician, and he came. The sick were isolated and tended carefully until death.

Meanwhile other European volunteers came forward, and one of them, Albert West, a printer, was dispatched to edit *Indian Opinion,* a paper Gandhi had started for discussing subjects that were both timeless and timely. After the plague was over, West reported that the finances of the periodical were in disorder, and Gandhi prepared to leave for Durban in Natal, where the paper was printed. Henry Polak went with him to the railway station, and as Gandhi entered the train he put into his hands a book by John Ruskin, a Briton who sought a simple and good life. Gandhi read it constantly during the twenty-four-hour train trip to Durban. He said, "The one book that brought about an instantaneous and practical transformation of my life was *Unto This Last.* . . . I discovered some of my deepest convictions reflected in this great book of Ruskin and that is why the book so captured me and made me transform my life. . . .

"This is how I understood Ruskin's teachings:

"*1. The good of the individual is contained in the good of all.*

28

"2. A lawyer's labor has the same value as the barber's, inasmuch as all have the same right of earning their livelihood from their labor.

"3. A life of labor, i.e., of a tiller of the soil and handcraftsman, is the life worth living. . . .

"I awoke with the dawn, ready to put these principles to practice."

This book set off the first of the great spiritual explosions of Gandhi's life. He went to see West, proposed that the paper and its staff be moved to a farm, where everyone should labor and where everyone should draw the same living wage. Within a week Gandhi purchased twenty acres of land in the country at a place called Phoenix, added eighty acres more, drew poor and well-to-do Indians and Europeans from their occupations, and established away from the cities and centers of temporal greatness the first of his ashrams, or communities for seeking after Truth. Thereafter he ate simple food, put on coarse clothes, lived in flimsy houses, and shared in the work of the scullery, the fields, and the latrines.

But there was not to be a life of quiet growth for Gandhi at his new ashram. Before long the authorities in the Transvaal put forth a new and onerous system of registration and fingerprinting for Asiatics and sought to increase the severity of the old laws. Their aim was to give color prejudice the full strength of law and to control the slave laborers while they pushed the freed laborers out of South Africa. Gandhi made clear to the people in the Transvaal that the government had taken the first step in evicting all Indians, and he proposed that a meeting be held on September 11, 1906, in the Old Empire Theatre in the city of Johannesburg to decide how Indians could maintain life in South Africa.

Out of this meeting came a second great spiritual explosion. Gandhi went to it without any settled ideas of what should be done. But he went to it with a deep experience of inner growth. Growth had begun in his youth, when he began to say the simple and primitive prayer of India, wherein the name of God is repeated until the very throat and lips become weary, so that he might banish his fears. Growth had gone forward during a period of reflection in London. It had been speeded up when his eyes fell upon the words of Jesus, ". . . I say unto you, resist not evil: but whosoever shall smite thee on thy right cheek, turn to him the other also. And if any man will sue thee at law to take away thy coat, let him have thy cloak also." His growth had been spurred by his talks in India with the poet Raychand, a saintly man of business whom Gandhi recognized as a seeker after Truth even before Gandhi knew what Truth was. And in South Africa growth had quickened and borne fruit. Gandhi was no longer the timid young man suffused with fear and shame. He had passed through beatings and through wars; he had led the Indian community in its struggle for simple human rights. He had sensed the depth of spirit of the great teachers of East and West; and he was already practicing what they had preached. He understood from his own life the commandment, "Love your enemies, bless them that curse you, do good to them that hate you, and pray for them which despitefully use you and persecute you, that ye may be sons of your Father which is in heaven." In his ears there were ever the verses of a Hindu poem:

*If a man gives you a drink and you give him a drink
in return, that is nothing.
Real beauty consists in doing good against evil.*

Although he sat on the platform of the Old Empire Theatre without anything ready to say, he was ready to say something. And when a Mussalman friend invoked the name of God in demanding an oath never to submit to registration, Gandhi got to his feet and called for a struggle for the rights of Indians that would rely entirely on the power of Truth, casting aside altogether the power of violence. He invited laborers, mineworkers, and merchants to disobey the government, to go to jail with their wives and sons and sisters if need be, to march in protest if need be, to leave work if need be, and in all cases to pray. He did not speak lightly of the danger, for he said:

"We may have to remain hungry and suffer from extreme heat and cold. Hard labor is likely to be imposed upon us in prison. We may even be flogged by the warders. Or we may not be imprisoned but fined heavily and our property attached and held up to auction for non-payment. Though some of us are wealthy today we may be reduced to poverty to-

31

morrow. We may even be deported from South Africa for good.

"Suffering from hunger and similar hardship in jail, some of us may fall ill or even die. Our wisdom, therefore, lies in pledging ourselves, knowing full well that we shall have to suffer things like these and even worse."

Then he spoke for himself, saying, "Even if everyone else were to hold back, leaving me alone, I am confident that I should never violate my pledge. Please do not misunderstand me. I am not suggesting this in a boastful spirit, but I wish earnestly to put you on your guard. I would respectfully suggest that if you have not the will or the ability to stand firm even when you are perfectly isolated, you should not only refuse to take the pledge yourselves but you should here and now declare your opposition to it. Each single man should fully realize his responsibilities and then only pledge himself independently of others. He should understand that he himself must be true to his pledge even unto death."

Then every man, Hindu, Mussalman, Parsi, and Christian, in the theater rose up and pledged to resist only by the power of Truth. This was the beginning of the great weapon of Satyagraha, according to which men conquer evil not by doing violence to others but by taking violence upon themselves.

4

In South Africa
he roused his fellow countrymen
and led them to non-violent victory
over those who tried violently
to keep them down.

For eight years the struggle against the British and Dutch in South Africa went on under a man who called upon those despised by the British and Dutch to defeat them with love. The people followed. There was no violence. Gandhi said not to register, and the government could persuade no more than five hundred out of some ten to fifteen thousand Indians in the Transvaal to disobey him. Gandhi told his followers to court jail deliberately, and they went out into the streets in great numbers and took to hawking without licenses until the jails shortly overflowed and tents were pitched outside them.

Gandhi himself was as active in jail as he had been out of it. He spaded soil in great heat until his hands became covered with oozing blisters. When the head jailer asked him for names of men to clean the latrines, Gandhi insisted that he do it himself. In the evenings he read the Bible and the Koran, English essays and Hindu scriptures. A young Chinese Chris-

33

tian wished to learn English, and Gandhi taught him the New Testament.

As the jails kept filling, the confusion of the government kept increasing, and, unable to win by force, it tried guile. It promised to repeal the old and onerous laws against Asiatics if the Indians would only register voluntarily. This promise for a time stirred up great trouble. Gandhi warned his countrymen that the promise might not be kept, but he insisted on trusting his adversary until there was no longer hope of trusting him.

Among the Indians there were those who wished to make no compromise at all, in particular a group of Pathan Mussalmans, a people much noted in India for honor and violence. As Gandhi went to have his fingerprints taken, one of the Pathans, a tall man by the name of Mir Alam, set upon him with a cudgel. Gandhi cried out, "Ai Rama," which means, "O God," and fell senseless upon the ground. Yet even before he would let his wounds be tended, he besought the government not to punish Mir Alam but to let him go. But the government would not.

Another day, on the way to a meeting, Gandhi left the side of a friend and walked over to a man by the edge of a porch. He linked arms with the man and they went down the street, whereupon an object changed hands. Seeing this exchange, the friend asked Gandhi, "What did the man want—anything special?"

Gandhi said, "Yes, he wanted to kill me."

The friend cried out, "The man is mad!"

34

But Gandhi said, "No, he is not mad, only mistaken; and you saw, after I had talked to him, he handed over the knife he had intended to use on me."

And he said later, "It is finished. I do not think the man will attempt to injure me again. Had I had him arrested, I should have made an enemy of him. As it is, he will now be my friend."

A little later the first assailant, Mir Alam, released from prison, rose to his feet in a public place to announce that he had done great wrong in attacking Gandhi.

Since the government did not keep its promises after all, and did not repeal the old laws, Gandhi called for a mass burning of the certificates that had been voluntarily taken out. Again the Indians courted jail, and great numbers of them went out of the Transvaal so that they might enter it illegally and fill up the jails once again. But the European leaders of South Africa wished at all costs to hold the color bar, and it was clear that the struggle would become a long one. The families of those in jail had to be supported, together with the prisoners themselves at such times as they were free. The farm at Phoenix was far away from the Transvaal. Gandhi no longer had any possessions to draw on, for he had given up money and law as obstacles to the taking of duties and risks and had decided to live out his life in poverty.

Then there came forward a well-to-do friend, Hermann Kallenbach, who gave over a farm of eleven hundred acres close to Johannesburg, and the second Gandhi ashram, or religious community, came into being. Gandhi called it Tolstoy Farm and with high faith made it a center of spiritual training for political struggle. He made it also a place of experiment. He experimented with the ways of the spirit as tirelessly and as widely as scientists experiment with the ways of nature. Here he tried out methods of teaching young people the techniques of labor and the truths of religion; and here he first undertook to make a new use of the practice of fasting, which is an old Hindu device of self-purification. The Hindu religion has long held that the body and its desires are evil and that the reducing of desires is good. Gandhi practiced fasting in order to take upon himself the misdeeds of others and suffer for them. At the ashram he also worked long and hard on natural treatments of illness. His faith shone out from him and gave strength to those who were about him. In four years there were no cases of serious illness.

This great soul did not talk harshly and with noise. His voice was quiet with affection, and it laughed with joy. He asked of others only what he had already done himself. He did not ask of any man anything far distant from that man's inward growth, for he knew from his own experience that Truth moves more often like rain sinking into soil than like lightning striking a tree. Besides—and this was his genius —Gandhi saw Truth as it lives here and now, and he refused to put it forth as an unbending set of laws. This great soul could indeed be followed, for he set an example not of unreachable final Truth but of outreaching growth toward the Truth that is in all men.

36

Meanwhile the struggle continued, and in 1912 the government again made promises. But nothing came of them but increased bitterness, in the midst of which it was decreed that all Hindu and Mussalman marriages were illegal everywhere in South Africa. Thus wives were made concubines, and children became illegitimates unable to inherit any property. Gandhi appealed to the government; he laid forth before the government his plans for a new Satyagraha. But the government would not listen. Thereupon Gandhi sent out his non-violent armies.

There was an army of men and women; there was even an army of women alone. Each army crossed from Natal into the Transvaal so that it might get itself arrested. While this resistance was being offered, more than five thousand laborers came out of the mines at Newcastle and trekked almost two hundred miles with Gandhi at their head into the Transvaal. Gandhi was arrested three times and released on bail twice, but the five thousand, some of them former murderers and robbers, did not give way to violence. They marched without complaint some ten days, whereupon the government arrested them all in a body.

At this, Indian laborers everywhere in South Africa went out from their work, some 60,000 of them, and the government called the military police to force them back. Many strikers who refused to give in were fired upon, and some were killed. The government began arresting everyone connected with Gandhi,

37

until the prison system started to cave in from the weight of the numbers of prisoners.

But of what use is imprisoning a man who is anxious to be imprisoned, and of what use is beating a man who is ready to be beaten, and of what use is shooting a man who is willing to die? These measures only built sympathy for Gandhi abroad and drew from the British Government in India a protest against the government in South Africa. The government saw that it must try new tactics and therefore named a commission. But Gandhi quickly proposed a new march unless the commission contained one member representing the Indians. The battle for a short time remained deadlocked. Then all at once Gandhi saw a chance for a great blow at the government.

For there suddenly broke out a railway strike of such violence and such size that it became almost an insurrection, and Gandhi was at once pressed to take advantage of it and start his new march. But he knew better the uses of Satyagraha. Refusing to take advantage of a situation not of the Indians' own making, he called off the new march altogether. At this act of goodness the government gave in completely, and the commission was instructed to meet all Indian demands. General Smuts, Gandhi's principal opponent, even became his admirer. The twenty-year battle was won.

Gandhi's work in South Africa was done. When he arrived back in India, the man who had left it timid and uncertain was already famous as a great soul, a Mahatma. This tremendous change-over, this giving

38

up of wealth for poverty, this abandonment of his own work for work for others, this discovery of new weapons of non-violence—none of this had come all at once. It had come from the daily change-overs of one who sought Truth, from the long, slow growth of one ready to gamble that Truth was active and alive in the world of men.

5

Home in India he taught Truth
in a community of all races and faiths,
practiced it locally, and made ready
to fight with it nationally.

In January 1915 the Great Soul came home to
a land crowded with three hundred fifty million people,
an empire, and a variety of maharajas, thakurs, and
nawabs. On this stage was played the great drama
in which the power of Truth, in the form of a scrawny
little man dressed in the loincloth of an untouchable,
was pitted against the powers of violence and selfishness of the world, in the form of viceroys, soldiers,
administrators, judges, and the beturbaned and sometimes bejeweled people of his own land.

Gandhi did not then nor did he at any time believe
that he had only to speak Truth in a loud voice from
the housetops and thereby save India. He was a man
who had only one aim, which was to experiment
humbly with Truth and seek to grow in it. He said,
"Man is a fallible being. He can never be sure of his
steps. What he may regard as an answer to prayer
may be an echo of his pride. For infallible guidance
man has to have a perfectly innocent heart, incapable
of evil. I can lay no such claim. Mine is a struggling,
striving, erring, imperfect soul. But I can rise only

by experimenting upon myself and others. I believe in the absolute oneness of God, and therefore also of humanity. What though we have bodies? We have but one soul. The rays of the sun are many through refraction. But they have the same source. I cannot, therefore, detach myself from the wickedest soul, nor may I be denied identity with the most virtuous. Whether, therefore, I will or not, I must involve in my own experiment the whole of my kind. Nor can I do without experiment. Life is but an endless series of experiments."

He said also: "If we are all sons of the same God and partake of the same divine essence, we must partake of the sin of every person, whether he belongs to us or another race."

Thus he put aside any thought that there was anything exceptional in him. But the people of India could not put that thought aside. Gandhi imagined that when his boat reached the city of Bombay he might be greeted by a few friends. He was greeted instead by great and unnumbered masses of people, crowding about the docks and the streets that they might see him. For in calling upon the weapons of Truth in South Africa, Gandhi had stirred the thoughts of the people in India. And in giving up a life of ease for a life of labor and poverty he had also stirred their hearts. Before he had done anything or said any word in India, the downtrodden had chosen him as one to whom they would listen and one whom they would follow.

· He never forgot the poor in goods and poor in

spirit. Love of God to him was not love until it led to life in their service, and although he was small and frail, given even to occasional illness, he put himself into prison for them, starved himself for them, and yet had the strength to edit papers, write books, direct battles, outwalk every morning men half his years, pray without ceasing, and talk to whoever sought him.

This was the situation in India: The British, who owned the land and ruled it, had come there not so much to live or to teach as to exploit. (Until a mutiny in 1857 the country was governed by a commercial company.) The greatness of India, however, was the greatness of religion, of architecture, and of the arts of the handicraftsman. For many thousands of years Indians had understood God as the One always present in the midst of the many, and they made their faith a way by which men could seek the One without hindrance or dogma. The Hindu religion was a great reservoir of the findings of men who had sought Truth, who had tried to lose their lives to save them, and who had made clear, more than the sages of any other country, man's need to grow in actual and living experience of Deity.

But how could the British in India understand this greatness? Almost all of them were administrators or soldiers or publicists, not philosophers or students, and almost all of them believed England superior in everything. One of them said that ". . . there are no books on any subject which deserve to be compared with our own. . . ." They were a caste apart, and most of them took a low view of natives. When they dealt with them in schools or in courts or in offices, they insisted that the English language was the only possible language and that English customs were the only possible customs. They brought railways and factories to India, but in general they brought them to take wealth out of the country, not to add well-being to it. The people of India, too numerous for the land they lived upon, were not only impoverished but broken in spirit. Gandhi said, "Only a free India can worship the true God," for he saw that foreign rule kept his people from manliness.

But Gandhi saw also the evils that India had put upon herself. That great country had fallen into a time of barrenness of spirit even before the coming of the British, and although there could be no real fertility of spirit while the country was enslaved to outsiders, yet there could be none while the people within the country were themselves weak and inert. Besides weakness, there was also evil. The country was of two faiths, a majority being Hindus and a minority Mussalmans, and from time to time the friction of difference brought terrible explosions of looting and bloodshed. As for the Hindus, they were so given to caste that they condemned the untouchables to the dirtiest of jobs and to the meanest of living places. And everywhere there was the evil of richness and poorness, for the gulf between the two was great. The richest men in the world lived in India, and so did the poorest.

Mahatma Gandhi saw all of these evils, and he

43

heard the voice of the people speaking his name.)
Thus seeing and thus hearing, he did not rush into
politics. Instead, he started another religious community, an ashram.

Gandhi knew the strength of community, wherein
men who live together seek Truth more fruitfully
than do men living separately. For when men search
as a group, the total of what they find is greater than
the sum of what they could have found alone. Gandhi
looked for nourishment from local roots, experimenting with Truth not from some vague place in space-
time, but in a particular place, a village or an ashram;
and he knew that love warms only when its hidden
brilliance falls on those near at hand. For what good
is it if a man loves ten thousand people ten thousand
miles off and cannot love his neighbor? Gandhi saw
Truth centering not in the great places of high government, but in the towns and the villages, and he
chose not to be footloose but footbound, so that he
might have fresh life from those whom it was given
for him to live with. He said, "We are departing from
one of the sacred laws of our being when we leave our
neighborhood and go out somewhere else in order
to satisfy our wants." He himself went to the farmers
and the merchants and the barbers near at hand, and
not those far away. Similarly he held onto his own
Hindu religion and did not seek to embrace any
other, saying in explanation that one's own religion
is like one's own wife.

He called his community the Satyagraha Ashram,

44

and he placed it outside Ahmedabad, a city near the place of his birth.

As in South Africa, so in India, his ashram was not exclusive; it was for all men. It was not only for Hindus, Mussalmans, Jews, and Christians, but also for those whom the Hindus treated as defiled. Shortly after the ashram was opened, an untouchable couple with a small child came to live there. The people of the ashram lived always as one family, and thus there was for a time not only strain inside the ashram but a great stir of prejudice on the outside, and those who supported the ashram cut off both money and water.

The treasurer of the ashram came to Gandhi and said, "We are out of funds, and there is nothing for the next month."

Gandhi replied quietly, "Then we shall go to the untouchable quarters." And he determined that if the ashram could not be continued he would take his community and live as brothers with those whom the pious would not look at as men. But at the last minute a moneylender, whom Gandhi remembered meeting only once before, drove up to the ashram and left 13,000 rupees.

When he first undertook to show other men how to live, it was natural that Gandhi should first of all take thought of his own community. He did not give them any dogma or creed or belief purely of the mind. He even kept insisting that he was not one who taught Truth but only one who sought to practice

45

it, but his practice overflowed into teaching. Gandhi himself had experienced the vanities and the temptations of the world, and by this experience he felt himself not drawn apart from but drawn together with both the brotherhood of good and the brotherhood of evil. He had experienced the great wonder of his own growth. And finally he had experienced Truth itself, hearing it alike in the silence of prayer and in the noise of the streets, hearing it and following it as all men can hear and follow but as few have actually heard and actually followed. What he taught was his own life, and his life brimmed over into words that point to Truth without indicating it, that suggest it without defining it. For the reality of his life was beyond words, even as Truth is beyond them.

First he explained Truth to the people of his ashram, saying that it is "not simply as we ordinarily understand it, not truth which merely answers the saying, 'Honesty is the best policy,' implying that if it is not the best policy we may depart from it, . . . We may have to rule our life by the law of Truth at any cost."

Then he told the story of the son who was in the right and the father who was in the wrong. "For the sake of Truth, he dared to oppose his father; and he defended himself, not by paying his father back in his own coin. Rather, in defense of Truth as he knew it, he was prepared to die without caring to return the blows that he received from his father . . . with the result that at last Truth rose triumphant. Not that he suffered the tortures because he knew that some day

46

or other in his very lifetime he would be able to demonstrate the infallibility of the law of Truth. That fact was there; but if he died in the midst of tortures, he would still have adhered to Truth. That is the Truth which I would like to follow."

In explaining the power of Truth in the world of men he said, "It really means that you may not offend anybody; you may not harbor an uncharitable thought, even in connection with one who may consider himself to be your enemy. To one who follows this doctrine there is no room for an enemy. But there may be people who consider themselves to be his enemies. So it is held that we may not harbor an evil thought even in connection with such persons. If we return blow for blow we depart from the doctrine of non-violence. But I go further. If we resent a friend's action, or the so-called enemy's action, we still fall short of this doctrine. But when I say we should not resent, I do not say that we should acquiesce; by the word 'resent' I mean wishing that some harm should be done to the enemy; or that he should be put out of the way, not even by any action of ours, but by the action of somebody else, or, say, by divine agency."

He said also, "This doctrine tells us that we may guard the honor of those under our charge by delivering our own lives into the hands of the man who would commit the sacrilege. And that requires far greater courage than delivering of blows. If you do not retaliate, but stand your ground between your charge and your opponent, simply receiving the blows without retaliating, what happens? I give you my

47

promise that the whole of his violence will be expended on you, and your friend will be left unscathed."

At the same time, Gandhi was preaching the equality of all people, and he believed that faith was not true faith if it did not seek to transform the outward ordering of life and to supplant the laws of rank with the rule of love. He would have nothing to do with the luxuries made by the poor for the rich, and he decried love of things for their own sake. Thus he proposed to the people of his ashram a vow of nonthieving, saying:

"I suggest that we are thieves in a way. If I take anything that I do not need for my own immediate use and keep it, I thieve it from somebody else. It is the fundamental law of Nature, without exception, that Nature produces enough for our wants from day to day; and if only everybody took enough for himself and nothing more there would be no pauperism in this world; there would be no man dying of starvation. I am no Socialist, and I do not want to dispossess those who have got possessions; but I do say that personally those of us who want to see light in darkness have to follow this rule. I do not want to dispossess anybody. I should then be departing from the rule of non-violence. If somebody else possesses more than I do, let him. But so far as my own life is regulated, I dare not possess anything which I do not need. In India we have got many millions of people who have to be satisfied with one meal a day, and that meal consisting of bread without yeast. You and I have no right to anything until these many millions are clothed and fed."

And he taught many other things besides. He taught men that they should be fearful of God in order not to be fearful of men and so to follow Truth. He taught men that politics have no meaning without Truth. Some of what he taught speaks more to the condition of Indians than to the condition of persons elsewhere in the world, for those parts of his teaching had to do with an asceticism in food and sex, an asceticism which did not believe that God could be worshiped by friends joining at meat or by husbands and wives coming together in love. But the center of his teaching was as broad as a sun which shines upon all things. That center was the light hidden within life, present whether men see it or not, but, for those who see it, the very source of power to strive against the evil of one's self and thus the evil of one's world.

How, then, could Gandhi keep long out of politics? He wrote once, "To see the universal and all-pervading Spirit of Truth face to face one must be able to love the meanest of creatures as oneself. And a man who aspires after that cannot afford to keep out of any field of life. That is why my devotion to Truth has drawn me into the field of politics; and I can say without the slightest hesitation and yet in all humility that those who say that religion has nothing to do with politics do not know what religion means." He wrote also, "An ounce of practice is worth tons of preaching."

49

In the year 1917 a man came to Gandhi begging that he would see with his own eyes the plight of the tenants and workers on the indigo plantations at Champaran. When Gandhi went, he at once began to look at the facts, as was his habit, and to study them. He also took steps to set up schools to relieve the sickness and ignorance of the people. At this the government became fearful and ordered him to go out of the place, but he went on with his inquiry. When the government arrested him for disobeying orders, he readily admitted disobedience and openly claimed obedience to the higher orders of conscience. Then the peasants of Champaran became greatly aroused and took to non-violence, and the government had to reconsider in haste. Gandhi's inquiry went on, and before long the government ordered that the evils that had been done the peasants be removed.

In the same year workers at the cotton mills at Ahmedabad came to Gandhi to learn how Satyagraha could be used in a labor strike, for their wages were low. For them Gandhi planned a new kind of strike, one which would overcome the employers by the power of Truth and not by fear or force or loss of money. He instructed the strikers not to molest any strikebreakers and never to use any violence. He insisted that they pledge themselves to take no charity and to remain firm in their suffering no matter how long the strike lasted. But after three weeks of the strike some of the men weakened and went back to work. Then Gandhi said that because he had urged the strikers to take their pledge, he himself must find some way of taking upon himself the evil of their breaking it, and he declared, "Unless the strikers rally and continue the strike till a settlement is reached, or till they leave the mills altogether, I will not touch any food." But how could anyone permit Gandhi to suffer in this way? The strikers became firm and the mill owners suddenly became weak. An agreement was reached without bitterness.

The next year Satyagraha was offered in the district of Khaira, which was suffering from a famine. Most of the farmers were unable to pay taxes without mortgaging all that they owned. They petitioned the government according to law, but the government would not listen. Then Gandhi told them that they must make ready to suffer loss of land, home, and cattle, but that they must not co-operate with the government or pay, any of them, any part of their taxes. The government began seizing property and it even beat some of the farmers, but the people of Khaira stood firm and non-violent, and aid for their struggle began to come in from their neighbors. Then the government gave in, and insisted only on saving face and collecting taxes from a few well-to-do farmers.

What had thus been shown in a few places was seen shortly all over India. The country had made large contributions of men and goods to England during World War I, and the people thought that their country would receive the status of a dominion as a reward. Gandhi, out of loyalty to Britain and out of hope for India, had even gone about urging

51

enlistments for war, taxing his strength and straining his convictions until his health broke and he was brought close to death. But dominion status was not granted. India became restive, and when the British marked this restiveness, they passed an act that limited the people's speech and assembly and gave the government the right to imprison anyone without trial.

Gandhi felt his loyalty shaken. He protested the act, but nothing came of his protesting, and he therefore called upon all India to fight the act with Satyagraha. Accordingly, work of all sorts came to a stop for a day, and the people gathered in great meetings and marched in great parades, pledging disobedience. But the government struck back with violence, and in some of the cities soldiers fired into the crowds. In the province of Punjab the people became troubled and gave way to acts of violence. Gandhi was asked to come quiet them, but the government would not allow it and arrested Gandhi and two local leaders. When a meeting of the people to protest the arrests was held at the city of Jallianwala Bagh, a British general named Dyer ordered machine gunners to fire, even though the people were peaceful. More than a thousand persons were killed and more than three thousand were wounded. General Dyer proclaimed that he had acted to produce a "moral effect." In England a testimonial fund of more than $100,000 was raised for him. In India there followed public floggings, and men in the Punjab were forced to cross a certain street crawling upon their bellies.

While this act was outraging all India, another act

was outraging the Mussalmans in particular. The British had promised during the war that the spiritual place of Turkey and of the Mussalman holy cities would be upheld, but the promise was not kept. This was called the Khilafat question, and Gandhi made common cause with the Mussalmans. One day in 1920 he spoke to a meeting in the city of Allahabad, and in the course of the talk it came to him that he should propose non-co-operation with the British until India was free and the wrongs against the Mussalmans were righted. For he could no longer believe that the British Empire practiced the equality of races, and he could no longer be loyal. He cried out, "Better for me a beggar's bowl than the richest possessions stained by the innocents of Jallianwala. Better by far a warrant of imprisonment than honeyed words from those who have wounded the religious sentiments of my seventy million brothers."

He thought thus about Britain: "By a long and prayerful discipline I have ceased for over forty years to hate anybody. I know that this is a big claim. Nevertheless I make it in all humility. But I can and I do hate evil wherever it exists. I hate the system of government that the British people have set up in India. I hate the domineering manner of Englishmen as a class in India. I hate the ruthless exploitation of India even as I hate from the bottom of my heart the hideous system of untouchability for which millions of Hindus have made themselves responsible.

"But I do not hate the domineering Englishmen, as I refuse to hate the domineering Hindus. I seek to reform them in all the loving ways that are open to me."

These loving ways were the ways of Satyagraha, and shortly Gandhi waged war upon the British all over India with the weapons of Truth.

6

*The first great struggle of non-violence
against the British almost succeeded,
but violence appeared.
Gandhi halted the struggle.
The British put him in jail.*

The start of the first great campaign against
the British was like the start of all Gandhi's struggles,
for it began with an appeal to the adversary and a
placing of all plans before him. Gandhi wrote to the
British viceroy, who was in all things the ultimate
power in India, returning all the medals given for his
co-operation with the British in South Africa, and
saying, "Events that have happened during the past
month have confirmed me in the opinion that the
Imperial Government has acted in the Khilafat matter
in an unscrupulous, immoral, and unjust manner, and
have been moving from wrong to wrong in order to
defend their immorality. I can retain neither respect
nor affection for such a government. . . . I have,
therefore, ventured to suggest the remedy of non-
co-operation, which enables those who wish to do so
to dissociate themselves from the government, and
which, if it is unattended by violence and undertaken
in an orderly manner, must compel it to retrace its
steps and undo the wrongs committed."

55

At once, all over India, men began giving up the honors and titles with which they had been invested. People ceased using the courts. The students and their professors went out of the government schools, leaving them deserted; government workers resigned from their jobs; and soldiers quit the army. Even the wealthy stopped subscribing to government loans. Thus the entire system of government was suddenly caught in paralysis.

This was the year 1921, and Gandhi had come to the age of fifty-two years, but he did not hold back his strength and retire to some central place and issue orders. In action he was as tireless as he was in prayer. Sometimes sick and sometimes well, he drove himself day after day, meeting and speaking to massed thousands, talking to friends and to political workers, directing drives, working up tactics, going out into the midst of the people to quiet them at the very time of violence, traveling all over India, and at the same time seeing anyone who wished to talk to him, editing magazines, composing articles, and writing dozens of letters each day. He wrote letters to the great and important in the struggle for freedom, and he wrote letters also to the unimportant, showing as much concern for the treatment of a friend sick in the ashram as for the next maneuver of non-co-operation against the British. He slept some four hours a night. He put himself completely into the battle, and as he moved over India a great change took hold of the people, for they saw a light in the midst of the darkness of their confusion and weakness. This man's total faith in the power of Truth, his humility before God and yet his confidence that God had called him to cure India's wounds—this faith shone throughout the land, and the many millions obeyed him. His outward activity was the harvest of his inward prayer, wherein he drew upon the power of Truth and ever came forth fresh.

A vast quickening came upon the country, and things that once would have taken centuries happened overnight. So intensely did the struggle burn that there were great changes in local habits, whole places giving up opium smoking, cities ridding themselves of prostitution, and many towns forsaking the oppression of untouchables. Hindus and Mussalmans, theretofore divided, drew closer together. The pressure upon the British system of government grew intense, and officials began to fear that Gandhi was within a stroke of forcing Britain out of India altogether.

This final stroke was indeed planned; it was the cutting off of the government from all sources of money, by way of mass refusal to pay any taxes or to buy any government materials, such as salt.

But there came a great and tragic moment. The entire country was aroused, and non-violence was almost completely practiced, but violence finally appeared beyond mistake in the ranks of the people. It was not the first violence among those pledged to non-violence, for blood had been shed two years earlier during the struggle over the acts limiting personal rights. In that violence Gandhi had even then seen a warning. For he described his offering of Satyagraha at that time as a "Himalayan miscalcu-

57

lation," and fasted to do penance. But that penance had not worked sufficiently deep. At the end of 1921 rioting broke out in Bombay, and shortly thereafter a number of policemen who had been provoking a crowd were hacked to pieces and burned in a place called Chauri Chaura.

To Gandhi it was unimportant that the violence was relatively slight or that it was provoked by the violence of the opponent, for violence is not excused by the degree of it or provocation of it. Gandhi had put his hand to the weapons of spirit to fight against evil, but he would not let evil be fought in any part by evil, and with sadness of heart and contrition of spirit he called off the non-co-operation campaign altogether. A country on the pinnacle of victory all at once found itself in the abyss of self-defeat.

Gandhi was overcome. He wrote, "We dare not enter the kingdom of liberty with mere lip homage to Truth and non-violence. . . . Suspension of mass civil disobedience and subsidence of excitement are necessary for further progress. . . . Let the opponent glory in our humiliation, or so-called defeat. It is better to be charged with cowardice and weakness than to be guilty of denial of our oath, and sin against God. It is a million times better to appear untrue before the world than to be untrue to ourselves." He cried out that he must undergo personal cleansing so that he might become a fitter vehicle of Truth, and he fasted five days.

Then there fell upon him the anger and the reproaches of many of his followers, some of whom had been using Truth not because it was true but because it was good policy. But although Gandhi was attacked and humiliated, he would not forsake Truth, and instead of criticizing the British he criticized himself and his followers. A deep depression settled upon the minds of the people, not only in the cities but in the villages, and the British took advantage of it to arrest Gandhi for promoting disaffection.

Before the British court Gandhi argued both Britain's evils and his own mistakes. He pleaded guilty to disaffection, and he said, "But I hold it to be a virtue to be disaffected toward a government which in its totality has done more harm to India than any previous system. . . . Holding such a belief, I consider it to be a sin to have affection for the system. . . . I am here, therefore, to invite and submit cheerfully to the highest penalty that can be inflicted upon me for what in law is a deliberate crime and what appears to me to be the highest duty of a citizen."

The judge replied, "It would be impossible to ignore the fact that, in the eyes of millions of your countrymen, you are a great patriot and a great leader. Even those who differ from you in politics look upon you as a man of high ideals and of noble and of even saintly life." Then he sentenced him to six years' imprisonment.

7

After he had come out of jail,
Gandhi struggled to heal India's own ills,
abandoning politics and traveling
everywhere over the land.

The light which had been confined could not be put into darkness, for India still saw the fact of Gandhi even if it did not see his presence. In the midst of the lowness of spirit that followed the end of the first great struggle, it was still evident that India had come out of sleep, and that her depression was but the uncertainty of one suddenly conscious but not yet fully awake. By deepening India's faith in Truth, Gandhi had aroused India's faith in herself.

Into Yeravda Prison itself there came a freshness of spirit, for prisoner Gandhi was as kindly and as gently humorous with those who confined him as he had been when free with those who had followed him. As his followers had loved him, so did his jailers. At the end of two years he fell sick with appendicitis, and after a British surgeon had operated on him, the whole magic of his being seemed to be set free. His keepers, his nurses, and his doctor cared for him with warmth and affection, as if he were a guest of honor instead of a prisoner of state.

A month after the operation he was released from

the prison, and he went into the town of Juhu to set about regaining his health. But what chance could he have for quiet? Before long people came to him telling of the plight of the untouchables in a town in the south of India called Vykom. In this place the outcastes were not only kept at a distance and forbidden the temples and certain better-caste areas, but even forbidden the main street, so that when they went from one place to another they had to make a long circuit. The people appealed to Gandhi to offer Satyagraha against the high castes so that the evil, which had already lasted many centuries, might be cured.

How could Gandhi say no to the requests? He had said, "If untouchability is a necessary part of Hinduism, I am not a Hindu." He had adopted an untouchable child as his own daughter. And he had written: "I abhor with my whole soul the system which has reduced a large number of Hindus to a level less than that of beasts. . . . Has a beast any mind or business but that of his master's? Has a panchama [an untouchable] a place he can call his own? He may not walk on the very roads he cleans and pays for by the sweat of his brow. He may not even dress as others do. . . . It is an abuse of language to say that we Hindus extend any toleration toward our panchama brothers. We have degraded them and then have the audacity to use their very degradation against their rise."

Gandhi therefore agreed to direct the Satyagraha at Vykom from his sickbed. He proposed that one of his followers walk with an untouchable over the road

61

that was forbidden. The two men obeyed, and they were beaten by the people of high caste. They walked again, and they were put into prison. Then a great number of people began walking, and they were arrested until there was no more space in the prisons, whereupon the authorities put a barrier across the road and stationed military police.

Then Gandhi directed that his followers stand day and night in front of the police in an attitude of prayer and plead with them. They stood thus for more than a year. The hot sun beat upon them, and at one time there came floods, so that the water stood waist high in the streets, but no one abandoned his post.

Gandhi would not allow any help from outside Vykom, for he knew that if a local problem were not locally solved, it would not be solved at all, but would break out afresh. And when his followers wrote to him their sadness over the long fruitlessness of the struggle, he replied that the local legislature might fail them, that he might fail them, but that God would never fail them or put upon them that which they could not endure. "I may wipe their tears," he said, "but suffering is their sole privilege. . . . The Vykom Satyagraha is the argument of suffering. The hardest heart and the grossest ignorance must disappear before the rising sun of suffering without anger and without malice."

After a time the suffering began to melt the prejudice of the people of the high castes. First they tried to argue that their prejudice was right. Then they brought food and clothing to those who were fighting against them. Finally they gave in, saying, "We cannot resist any longer the prayers that have been made to us, and we are ready to receive the untouchables." The roads were opened, not only in Vykom but in many other places throughout India.

All the time Truth was being waged in Vykom, Gandhi was struggling to bring unity between Hindus and Mussalmans. For at the end of the campaign of non-co-operation small politicians came out of their places of hiding and began to salt the old wounds of religious difference, and while Gandhi was in jail the wounds began to fester and break. The villages remained quiet, but in the larger places there were bloodshed, looting, and outrage.

Gandhi sought first of all to find out the facts of each outbreak, for bitterness produced false reports. Then he pleaded with each side to tolerate the customs of the other, pointing out that "Each community should put its own house in order without bargaining with the other," and he said that the people would not fight if the leaders would not. Finally he advised the people of his own faith, the Hindus, to give in to Mussalman demands altogether, for he could not tolerate the idea of one side trying to wring concessions out of the other. He believed that the Mussalmans should be won over, not forced over, and he reminded Hindus that theirs was the most tolerant of religions, saying:

"As I write these lines, I feel a crowd of sectarians whispering to me, 'That is no Hinduism you are de-

63

fining; come to us and we will show you the Truth.' I am confounding all these whisperers by saying *Neti Neti,* 'not that, my friends, not that'; and they make confusion worse confounded by retorting with redoubled fury, 'Not that, not that.' But still another voice whispers to me, 'Why all this dueling—this war of words? I can show you a way out of it. It lies through silent prayer.'"

But the violence and outrage went on, and distress grew in Gandhi's mind. He thought within himself that he had been an instrument in awakening the energies of the people, and that he must find the remedy now that the energies were becoming self-destructive. He asked himself, "Have I erred, have I been impatient, have I compromised with evil? I may have done all these things or none of them. All I know is what I see before me. If real non-violence and Truth had been practiced by the people who are now fighting, the gory dueling that is now going on would have been impossible. My responsibility is clearly somewhere."

Many nights Gandhi rose in prayer to ask what he might do. On September 17, 1924, the answer came to him like a flash, and the next day, without consulting anyone, he announced: "The recent events have proved unbearable for me. My helplessness is still more unbearable. My religion teaches me that whenever there is distress which one cannot remove, one must fast and pray. . . . Nothing evidently that I can say or write can bring the two communities together. I am therefore imposing on myself a fast of twenty-one days commencing today and ending on Wednesday, October 6. . . . It is both a penance and a prayer."

Gandhi's fasts were undertaken not by way of protest, but by way of self-examination and purification. This man of goodness took upon himself the evils of his country in order to rid himself and the country of them. "I find," he said, "that my words have lost their power, which to me means there is something wrong with me and God has deserted me. I am fasting and praying that God may come back to me and restore effect to my words."

And he said of his fast that "It is a warning to the Hindus and Mussalmans who have professed to love me. If they have loved me truly and I have been deserving of their love, they will do penance with me for the grave sin of denying God in their hearts. To revile one another's religion, to make reckless statements, to utter untruth, to break the heads of innocent men, to desecrate temples or mosques, *is* a denial of God. . . . I ask no Hindu or Mussalman to surrender one iota of his religious principle. Only let him be sure that it is his religion. But I do ask of every Hindu and Mussalman not to fight for an earthly gain. I should be deeply hurt if my fast made either community surrender on a matter of principle. My fast is a matter between God and myself."

All this time Gandhi lay in the house of a Mussalman friend outside the city of Delhi. He had not yet recovered his health after his operation, and friends, fearful of his life, came to him and argued that he break the fast, urging that he take thought of the consequences to himself and to India. But while he talked gently with his arguers, he would not agree with them. On the twelfth day physicians feared that his life was in immediate danger, and friends pressed Gandhi again. But he wrote down on a slate, for it was a day of silence, "You have forgotten the power of prayer." And thereafter throughout the fast he kept healthy in body and spirit.

Outside, sensational stories of Hindu-Mussalman violence went out of the newspapers, and leaders of both groups hastily came together for a unity conference. For more than a year violence ceased. But the great results of the fast were hidden within the hearts of men and could never be made known.

This fast took place during the pause that must always follow a great effort. After he had called off the first campaign of non-co-operation, Gandhi said little about eventual freedom and much about current ills. He had sensed that a period of retreat was essential that the people might learn to experience Truth and non-violence in their own lives, and that violence might not again bring evil into the struggle for freedom. He knew that a man could not think violence against his neighbor and yet fight with the weapons of Truth against the British. Therefore he said that ". . . the struggle must, for the moment, be transformed to a change of heart among the Hindus and the Mussalmans. Before they dare think of freedom they must be brave enough to love one another, to tolerate one another's religion, even prejudices and superstitions, and to trust one another. This requires faith in oneself. And faith in oneself is faith in God. If we have that faith we shall cease to fear one another."

To develop that faith, he urged three things only. One was unity between Hindus and Mussalmans. The second was the casting out of untouchability. The third was simple labor, and he made the spinning wheel the great symbol of it. India once had had small industries in the cottages of its farmers and villagers, of which the most productive was the spinning of cotton grown in the fields; but the people had let foreign machine cloth push out their own cloth, and they therefore lacked ways of adding to their meager earnings from the land. Gandhi, consequently, undertook to bring spinning back into Indian life. He reasoned that spinning was easy and the wheel inexpensive, that it was still known and understood by the people, and that it would appeal to their feelings. He knew that homespun yarn would save money otherwise sent out of the country, and that it would spread the money among those who most desperately needed it. He saw spinning also as an excellent way of entry into the 700,000 villages of India for rural teaching and reform. And he believed deeply that every man, no matter what his regular calling, should do some form of labor each day. Thus he not only took to an hour's spinning a day himself, but urged it upon all of his friends, his followers, and his co-workers.

He was not troubled that home spinning would cut the income of Indian as well as British mill owners. When complaints were made that he was bringing prosperity to the lower orders who lacked respectability and ruining a number of middle-class persons, he answered, "In what sense are they lower except in their poverty, for which we the middle class are responsible? . . . If the middle-class people voluntarily suffer losses for the sake of the 'lower classes,' it would be but tardy reparation for their participation in their exploitation."

All this while India was in awe of the person of Gandhi, but all this while Gandhi was attacked, and his teachings were misunderstood on one side and another. Wishing that his influence would decline, the British assured themselves that it had in fact declined. Revolutionists sent letters to him insisting that true patriots were those who used force. The people of high caste argued with him about loving untouchables. And there were many important people in India who were not particularly interested in villages, who preferred not to think overmuch about the Hindu-Mussalman troubles, and who did not, in any case, want to spend time on spinning. There were others who did not think of Truth and non-violence as a faith, but as a policy, for their eyes were forever centered on the one idea of independence from Britain.

Many of these persons were members of the Indian National Congress, a group active for independence. Gandhi had earlier joined this group, and he had changed it from a body of spiritless debaters into the leading force in the campaign of non-co-operation. During the period of pause after the campaign he continued as president of it. But at that time there was no immediate political struggle. Bickering broke out, and many men who were warm to Gandhi became lukewarm to his program. They knew that the masses of the people followed him solidly, but they were not the masses; nor could they grasp the inward source of his power. Gandhi said, "Most religious men I have met are politicians in disguise. I, however, who wear the guise of a politician, am at heart a religious man."

For Gandhi brought together in his own being two things that looked very much different but were actually very much alike—highly practical politics and highly exalted faith. His friends who differed from him were much less religious and not nearly so practical, and how could they understand him? They did not want anyone but Gandhi to lead them, but they could not always like the way they were led.

A time came when Congress approved certain parts of Gandhi's program by only a bare majority. But Gandhi did not believe in the power of a majority, but in the power of Truth. Therefore he refused to be led into quarrels, and he even refused to influence Congress on disputed questions. He encouraged his opposition to speak out freely. Then he surrendered to the opposition and handed them full freedom to run Congress as they wished. Finally in 1925 he retired

69

from the presidency of Congress and announced he would not talk politics for a year.

When this happened, men who believed in Gandhi's program were much upset, for they did not understand that the best way to win over a friendly opponent is to give in to him. And Gandhi told them that non-violence was nothing unless those who used it were willing to make compromises to gain unity. He said, "Moral authority is never retained by any attempt to hold on to it. It comes without seeking and is retained without effort."

Then he went off to visit the villages.

During the next few years Gandhi saw more of India than any man had seen before him. He went about on foot and by car and oxcart, talking about spinning, about brothering untouchables, and about keeping friendship between Hindus and Mussalmans. He established many ashrams all over the land for training the people in non-violence. In 1928 he kept watch on a rural Satyagraha in the district of Bardoli, which he gave to one of his lieutenants, Sardar Patel, to direct. In this battle farmers protesting a rise in taxes refused to pay them, went to jail, and finally left their homes in a body for a neighboring territory, thus paralyzing the government, which after five and a half months of violent counter-struggle had to give in.

Wherever Gandhi went, people flocked to him. He once addressed a crowd of one hundred thousand gathered to listen to him and look at an eclipse, and everyone forgot the eclipse. Such attention troubled him, and he kept on denying that there was anything unusual about him. When a well in Karadi, many years dry, suddenly put forth water when his feet first touched the soil of the village, the people came to him, bowed down, and said:

"We have come to worship you, for you must be an incarnation of God."

But he said to them, "That is foolish and unbecoming of you. I have no more influence with God than you have."

He was glad that he could speak to the people and yet troubled that they came to look at him. He often said, "I can profit by criticism, never by praise," and he repeated again and again that he was tired of Mahatma, but the people came to look at him because he was indeed a great soul. Once he was traveling between Bengalore and Madras, and at night a great mob surrounded the small railway junction of Jalarput with such enthusiasm and racket that no one could speak. "It was all well meant," Gandhi said, "it was all an exhibition of boundless love, yet how cruel, how unreasonable."

And he reported on another occasion: "Srijut Srinivas Aiyangar and I were attending a meeting in Madras. People were bubbling with enthusiasm. We were driving to keep time for another meeting. But my 'admirers' insisted on exhibiting me through a street which was not on the program. They pleaded; I pleaded want of time. Srijut Aiyangar pleaded on behalf of my health. It was all to no purpose. We were driven—shall I say compulsorily? Both of us realized

71

that these men were no help to the cause; they were a positive hindrance. Things were set right only when I took the law in my hands, declined to be driven, actually got out of the car, and defied the crowd to carry me bodily if they wished. . . . I can cite a score of such experiences."

The people wished to exhibit Gandhi as a god, but Gandhi said, "An expectant and believing people groaning under misery believe that I have a message for them. They come from all quarters within walking reach to meet me. I do believe that I have a message of hope and certain deliverance, but——? Yes, it is a big *but*. There is no deliverance and no hope without sacrifice, discipline, and self-control. Mere sacrifice without discipline will be unavailing. How to evolve discipline out of this habitual indiscipline?"

8

Gandhi knew that Truth is in all men,
making them one. During the years
of traveling he taught three things:
Truth, non-violence, simplicity.

His teaching of Truth during these years was
not set down in a block of words, nor was it spoken
in a series of sermons. Gandhi did not sit down under
a tree or stand up in a building and talk of Truth as
something off by itself. Instead, he went walking
through the villages talking about practical matters
of poverty and tolerance. When he stood up in the
towns and the cities to speak, he said the same things,
and it was these same things that he wrote down in his
paper, *Young India*. Yet all the time he was talking
about Truth. He did not speak of things near by in
terms of the far distant, but of things far distant in
terms of the near by. And all the while he was speaking in this way to India the outside world overheard.

The world did not hear any message in which one
thought followed another thought according to plan.
It heard straws of thoughts and wisps of ideas in
great profusion—for if all Gandhi's words were put
down they would fill many books—but in some manner these wisps and straws fell by themselves into a

73

single message and into one Truth. This is the essence of what was heard during those years:

"Things in this world are not what they seem and do not seem as they really are. Or if they are seen as they are, they so appear only to a few who have perfected themselves after ages of penance. But none has yet been able to describe the reality, and no one can."

". . . If we are, God is. . . . If God is not, we are not."

Truth, therefore, is that which is not at any time seen but at all times felt, and it is known even by those who say that they have never known it. For if a man says that he has nothing to do with Truth, he is like a man who breathes and yet says that there is no air.

Gandhi taught the people, saying, "I do simply perceive that whilst everything is ever-changing, ever-dying, there is underlying all that change a Living Power that is changeless, that holds all together, that creates, dissolves, and re-creates. That in-forming Power or Spirit is God; and since nothing else that I see merely through the senses can or will persist, He alone is.

"And is this power benevolent or malevolent? I see it as purely benevolent. For I can see that in the midst of death, life persists; in the midst of untruth, truth persists; in the midst of darkness, light persists."

Gandhi spoke to the people further: "To me God is Truth and Love; God is ethics and morality; God is fearlessness; God is the source of Light and Life, and yet He is above and beyond all these. God is conscience. He is even the atheism of the atheist. For

74

in His boundless heart God permits the atheist to live. He is the searcher of hearts. He transcends speech and reason. He knows us and our hearts better than we do ourselves. He does not take us at our word, for He knows that we often do not mean it, some knowingly and others unknowingly.

"God is personal to those who need His personal presence. He is embodied to those who need His touch. He is all things to all men. He is in us and yet above and beyond us. . . .

"God cannot cease to be because hideous immoralities or inhuman brutalities are committed in His name. He is long-suffering. He is patient, but He is also terrible. He is the most exacting personage in the world and the world to come. He metes out the same measure to us that we mete out to our neighbors—men and brutes. With Him ignorance is no excuse. And withal He is ever-forgiving, for He always gives us the chance to repent. He is the greatest Democrat the world knows, for He leaves us unfettered to make our own choice between evil and good. He is the greatest Tyrant ever known, for He often dashes the cup from our lips and under cover of free will leaves us a margin so wholly inadequate as to provide only mirth for Himself at our expense. . . .

"Relief will come only when there is the least hope of it. For such is the way of that cruelly kind Deity who insists upon testing his devotees through a fiery furnace and delights in humbling them to the dust.

"Worship and prayer, therefore, are not to be per-

75

formed with the lips but with the heart. That is why they can be performed equally by the dumb and the stammerer, by the ignorant and the stupid; and the prayers of those whose tongues are nectared, but whose hearts are full of poison, are never heard."

He spoke not of any single religion but of all Truth. He did not think it necessary to go into churches, temples, and mosques. He said, "The answer to my prayer is clear and emphatic, that God is not encased in a safe to be approached through a little hole bored in it, but that He is open to be approached through millions of openings. . . ."

He said also, "I claim to be a man of faith and prayer, and even if I were to be cut to pieces I trust God would give me the strength not to deny Him, but to assert that He is. The Mussalman says, 'He is, and there is no one else.' The Christian says the same thing, and so does the Hindu. If I may venture to say so, the Buddhist also says the same thing, only in different words. It is true that we may each of us be putting our own interpretation on the word 'God.' We must of necessity do so; for God embraces, not only this tiny globe of ours, but millions and billions of such globes and worlds beyond worlds. How can we, little crawling creatures, possibly measure His greatness, His boundless love, His infinite compassion? So great is His infinite love and pity that He allows man insolently to deny Him, to wrangle about Him, and even to cut the throat of his fellow man!

"I confess that I have no argument to convince through reason. Faith transcends reason. All I can ad-

76

vise is not to attempt the impossible. I cannot account for the existence of evil by any rational method. To want to do so is to be co-equal with God. . . . I know that He has no evil in Himself; and yet if there is evil He is the author of it and yet untouched by it."

Gandhi saw evil as sharply as he saw good, and he saw it where it is, in each individual man. He said:

"I know, too, that I shall never know God if I do not wrestle with and against evil, even at the cost of life itself. . . . How much more should I be near Him when my faith is not a mere apology, as it is today, but has become as immovable as the Himalayas and as white as the snows on their peaks?"

Believing truthful things, Gandhi used the same things to fight against evil. He said, "The only way love punishes is by suffering." He said also, "There is only one fundamental Truth, which is Truth itself, otherwise known as non-violence. . . . I discovered in the earliest stages that pursuit of Truth did not admit of violence being inflicted upon one's opponent, but that he must be weaned from error by patience and sympathy. For what appears to be Truth to one may appear to be error to another."

For what good is it to hurt evil men? Truth is in all men, making them one, and not in a few of them, making them separate. To do hurt to any man is to do hurt to oneself, for to injure him is to injure Truth in him and thus to hurt the whole world. Nor is there good in forcing a man toward outward goodness by fear of injury, for evil is not only what men do to make other men suffer but what men think within themselves. "A man who broods on evil," Gandhi wrote, "is as bad as a man who does evil, if he is no worse." Therefore when violence is fought with violence it begets greater violence, and evil grows, and men are cast into slavery. Gandhi said: ". . . the light within me is steady and clear. There is no escape for any of us save through truth and non-violence. I know that war is wrong, is an unmitigated evil. I know, too, that it has got to go. I firmly believe that freedom won through bloodshed or fraud is no freedom. Would that all the acts alleged against me were found to be wholly indefensible rather than that, by any act of mine, non-violence was held to be compromised, or that I ever thought to be in favor of violence or untruth in any shape or form. Not violence, not untruth, but non-violence! Truth is the law of our being!"

But, hating evil, Gandhi would not let men run off from evil. He said, "Between violence and cowardly flight I can only prefer violence to cowardice. I can no more preach non-violence to a coward than I can tempt a blind man to enjoy healthy scenes. . . . As a coward, which I was for years, I harbored violence. I began to prize non-violence only when I began to shed cowardice. . . . A rabbit that runs away from the bull terrier is not particularly non-violent."

What shall men do if they can neither fight violently against evil nor yet run passively away from it? What Gandhi experimented with and what he demonstrated to men was the power of Truth, whereby one does not cause suffering to others but takes suffering upon oneself. For the Truth that is in men is touched by such suffering. "There is no one so fallen in this world," Gandhi said, "but can be converted by love." And he said many times, "He who believes in non-violence, believes in a living God." He drew no sharp line between this practical world of God's and that other timeless world of God's: A man who loses his life to save it, saves not only for that other world but for this one. Truth is not only active hereafter but active now, for now is a part of hereafter, and one spirit suffuses both. Therefore Gandhi said, "Self-sacrifice of one innocent man is a million times more potent than the sacrifice of millions of men who die in the act of killing others." "It does not mean meek submission to the will of the evildoer, but it means the putting one's soul against the will of the tyrant."

Therefore he declared, "If blood be shed, let it be our blood. Cultivate the quiet courage of dying without killing." "Non-violence is a weapon of the strong. With the weak it might easily be hypocrisy."

And in his own life and in his own words he showed that this self-sacrificing power of Truth could be used by men or women or children, that it could be used against the evils of a father or of an empire, the injustices of a neighbor or of a corporation. And he proved that, while other means sowed bitterness, the power of Truth alone reaped a spirit of unity, even in a world given over to turmoil.

79

"Whether mankind will consciously follow the law of love," he said, "I do not know. But that need not disturb us. The law will work just as the law of gravitation works, whether we accept it or not. The man who discovered for us the law of love was a far greater scientist than any of our modern scientists. Only our explorations have not gone far enough and so it is not possible for everyone to see all its workings."

Gandhi lived that he might make these explorations. When he saw evil he would not take part in it. When he saw injustice he would not work with it. When he saw untruth he would not stay beside it. But he would suffer against evil, sacrifice himself against injustice, and die against untruth. The Truth he loved was his weapon against what he hated. This was his exploration, his discovery, and his teaching.

But how can a man love Truth and use it if he worships possessions? How can he be one with his neighbors if he owns far more than they do? Gandhi said, "Money renders a man helpless." For he hated man's attachment to things, and he asked himself what man really needs. For what does he need besides garments to cover him, a house to shelter him, and food sufficient to keep him? He needs health. But what more does he need? Is a man made great by the competitive getting of things? Does he find Truth because he bathes in a porcelain tub instead of a wooden bucket? Does he know God because he owns furs, jewels, and large automobiles? "I say to you

. . . fly from that self-destroying show of Mammon which I see around me today. For you cannot serve Mammon and God together."

He told this story: "When a robber comes to take away A's property he can deliver the property to him if he recognizes in him a blood brother. If he does not feel like one but dreads the robber and would wish that someone was near to knock him down, he must try to knock him down and take the consequence. If he has the desire but not the ability to fight the robber, he must allow himself to be robbed and then call in the assistance of law courts to regain his lost property. In both cases he has as good a chance of losing his property as of regaining it. If he is a sane man like me, he would reach with me the conclusion that to be really happy he must not own anything or own things only so long as his neighbors permit him. In the last resort we live not by our physical strength but by sufferance."

Gandhi's city of Truth was not a great and diverse center of commerce and government. It was a simple community in which neighbors could seek unity. He did not want big industries but cottage industries; he did not want a strong government but strong communities. In fact, he wanted no government at all, for he wanted men to govern themselves—spinners, weavers, farmers, artisans, and traders, and not simply capitalists, lawyers, professors, politicians, and princes. He did not want such machinery and factories as would break the oneness of simple community life. He wanted to adapt machinery to

81

that life, and not change the life for the sake of the machinery. He said, "The machine should not be allowed to cripple the limbs of man."

He said, "Do not believe that multiplication of wants, and machinery contributed to supply them, is taking the world a single step nearer its goal. . . . I wholeheartedly detest this mad desire to destroy distance and time, to increase animal appetites, and to go to the ends of the earth in search of their satisfaction."

And to the same purpose he said, "Do not confuse Jesus' teaching with what passes as modern civilization."

Over against the mammon of automobiles, bathtubs, rich clothes, expensive houses, and many possessions he put the voluntary suffering of Jesus upon the cross. There was one picture on the walls of his mud hut. It was a picture of Jesus.

9

A second great struggle against
the British lasted three years
and ended with Gandhi in jail,
where he fasted
on behalf of the untouchables.

During the years of pause the spirit of India enlarged so that where she was once full of lethargy she became full of strength. When the British in 1928 sent out a commission under Sir John Simon without anyone on it to represent India, the country rose up in non-violent protest against it. The police charged down upon the people and beat them with batons and lathis, which are long bamboo clubs weighted at one end, but the people kept gathering and waving their banners, and they kept crying out the words, "Go back, Simon."

During this year some of the students became nettled over the non-violence of Gandhi, and some of them even hissed at him and booed. But he kept saying, "I would rather that India perish than that she won her freedom at the sacrifice of Truth."

And he said also, "Freedom is the gift of God, the right of every nation. . . . We may claim it, but if we claim it by methods repugnant to God, it will never be a blessing to us. We must win it by self-suffering. You must have no hate nor bitterness against the British. They are a fine people. It is only their system of government you must hate. You must honor and love them. You must see that not a hair of their heads is hurt. Rivers of blood may have to flow before we gain our freedom, but it must be our blood. We may not shed anybody else's."

In the same year of 1928 Congress resolved that if Britain's promise of dominion status were not kept within one year the country would struggle for full independence, and at midnight of December 21, 1929, Gandhi stood before Congress and read India's declaration of independence. Enthusiasm again covered the land; dissenters gave over their quibbling; and Indians drew together around Gandhi.

But before the struggle was joined, Gandhi wrote to the Viceroy, even as he had written in 1920, appealing to him and telling him his plans of battle. Again the Viceroy would do nothing, and Gandhi cried out, "On bended knees I asked for bread and received a stone. . . . The only public peace the nation knows is the peace of the public prison. I repudiate this law and regard it as my sacred duty to break the mournful monotony of compulsory peace that is choking the heart of the nation for want of free vent."

Gandhi settled upon the Salt Act as the first point of attack, for the making and selling of salt was a monopoly that brought income to the government and worked hardship on the people. Gandhi brought together the people of his own ashram, and he took a

vow not to live again in the place until India had
become free. Then, while all India watched him, he
marched off, staff in hand, at the head of his followers on a two hundred mile march to the sea, there to
make salt and break the law.

The British thereupon made plans to arrest him,
but they were full of fear. In the middle of the night
they stopped a train in the jungle near the place where
Gandhi was sleeping, and they sent officers, a magis-
trate, and many police to take him. The police
trembled and kept their hands on their revolvers,
but Gandhi was easy and laughing, and after singing
a song with his followers, he went briskly into the
police wagon.

Thereafter Satyagraha was let loose all over India.
Again the leaders and the people courted prison, and
again the prisons filled up, for in one year more than
100,000 persons, of whom many were women, went
to jail. When there was no more room in the jails, the
British forbade news to the newspapers and took
to violence, so that there followed many beatings and
shootings. But the people printed the news on hand-
bills and wrote it down in chalk on the pavements.
They kept refusing to obey unjust laws, and the
great processions did not leave the streets. When
pickets were beaten down, new pickets took their
places. Women everywhere came out of seclusion and
paraded and picketed. The people did not respond
to violence with violence. The work of the years
that had gone before made itself felt: volunteers
asked for blows with smiles on their faces and courte-

ous words on their lips, and even the Pathan Mussalmans, the violent and active men who lived on the frontier, held their peace when machine guns were fired into them and many hundreds of them were killed. For in this battle brave men were made humble and cowards were made strong; both suffered, and both held back from violence. Exactly at the time that Gandhi taught civil disobedience against the opponent he taught the much harder lesson of civility toward the opponent. And India saw that he had the power of making heroes from clay.

At the end of the year 1931 the government was paralyzed and worn out. The Congress leaders, therefore, were taken from the jails, and the Viceroy started negotiations with Gandhi. These talks did not please certain of the British, and in London Winston Churchill said, "It is alarming and also nauseating to see Mr. Gandhi, a seditious Middle Temple lawyer, now posing as a fakir of a type well known in the East, striding half naked up the steps of the Viceregal Palace while he is still organizing and conducting a defiant campaign of civil disobedience, to parley on equal terms with the representative of the King-Emperor."

But the negotiations went on, and Gandhi agreed to suspend civil disobedience in exchange for the repeal of the Salt Act and certain other unjust laws, and for promise of a new constitution for India. He even went to London to a round-table conference to discuss such a constitution. While there he wished to stay with his opponent, Winston Churchill, but

Churchill would not have him, and he stayed instead in a settlement house in London's East End, where the people gathered about him as they had gathered in India. Small children rose from their beds early to look at him, crowd next to him, and call him Uncle Gandhi.

During the time Gandhi was in England the British changed viceroys, and they soon began new acts of repression. Gandhi had not been back in India ten days before he was again arrested, and with him the more important of his followers. The entire Indian Congress itself and all of its educational branches—numbering thousands in each of many provinces—were declared illegal. Civil disobedience began once again, and it went on for two years, until gradually it quieted down and Gandhi put an end to it. But it did not end in defeat, for the British made concessions which, although incomplete, were yet great enough to make Congress the ruling body in most of the very provinces in which it had been formerly outlawed.

While the nation gradually relaxed after its second great effort, Gandhi took fresh strength and again raised the cry of brotherhood with the untouchables. During 1932, although he was still in prison, Gandhi began a new paper, *Harijan,* a word which means "God's own," and which Gandhi applied to the untouchables. In the same year the government put forth a law providing that Hindus without caste should elect representatives separate from other Hindus, and Gandhi declared that he would fast until death or until he had effected a change of heart in the government. After six days the government withdrew the law and signed a pact with him.

But Gandhi did not speak to the government alone, for he spoke to his countrymen, saying, "It is they [the so-called caste Hindus] who have to embrace the suppressed brothers and sisters as their own, whom they have to invite to their temples, to their homes, to their schools. The 'untouchables' in the villages should be made to feel that their shackles have been broken, that they are in no way inferior to their fellow villagers, and that they are worshipers of the same God as other villagers and are entitled to the same rights and privileges that the latter enjoy. But if the vital conditions of the pact are not kept by caste Hindus, could I possibly live to face God and man?"

A year later, when the pact had been kept, but only in part, he heard an unmistakable inner voice, and he settled upon another fast: "a heart prayer for purification of myself and my associates for greater vigilance and watchfulness in connection with the Harijan cause."

At this the British took fright, for they were too weak to bear the onus of Gandhi's dying in jail, and they released him on the second day of the fast. Gandhi continued his fast for the full twenty-one days that he had set, and at the end of it he took up fresh efforts against all prejudice.

10

During a second period of pause,
Gandhi went on with his teaching.
East and West looked at him,
followed him, and yet misunderstood him.

Again there was pause, again there was a period of retreat, again Gandhi left Congress altogether and went out among the villages in every part of India. In the first year after his leaving prison he fasted seven days to become more fit to overcome the prejudice he saw around him. In the second year he fasted again seven days because some of his followers attacked orthodox Hindus who were making a demonstration against him.

All this while he was without any fixed community, for he had vowed never to return to his ashram near Ahmedabad until India was free, and India was still far from free. But he did not wish to continue unrooted any longer, and so he set himself down at a place called Wardha in the center of India. At first he thought to live there without any followers, but he could not refuse anyone, and people came to him until he had again another ashram, which was called Sevagram.

For the next few years this was the main place of his teaching and work. From here he watched over the progress of Satyagraha as it was offered in various of the native states, for one part in five of the area of India was owned and ruled by maharajas, thakurs, and nawabs, native princes who were free to do whatever they liked so long as the British liked it.

One of the states in which Satyagraha was offered was Rajkot, where Gandhi had spent his youth. Here the thakur, after giving in to the non-violence practiced against his misrule, broke an agreement. When this happened, Gandhi proclaimed a fast to the death, but the fast did not last long, for the thakur was frightened and the British were alarmed so that all sides, overcome by the terrible power of meekness, rushed to support the agreement that they had previously conspired to break. And changes were made and reforms came into being in many of the native states.

These were the outward events of those years. But the great inward event was the teaching of the toothless little man armed outwardly with nothing mightier than deep eyes and a gentle smile.

There were many who could not understand that event. The people were at all times devoted to Gandhi, and they would not question anything he said, but they would not always understand all that he said to them. As for the better off, they were charmed by him, but many were also repelled by him. Such persons could not see that Truth must take root in men before it flourishes in the world, for they believed that the world should be this or the world should be that, according to their own wishes.

There were the orthodox, who looked backward to the settled orders of caste and family and wished that a renewed people might be confined in old vessels. There were also revolutionaries and reformers who had seen the ways of the West, and they wished that all sorts of new ways might be put upon India so that she might take upon herself the richness and modernness of powerful countries abroad. It was such men as Khan Abdul Ghaffar Khan, leader of the simple and rugged Pathan Mussalmans, who accepted non-violence most completely, and not the Hindus of high sophistication and great learning.

Many of these men wished to regulate life and have other men keep to the regulations, for they did not sense the inward workings of Truth. Yet even persons who did sense those workings misunderstood Gandhi. They thought Truth and non-violence must be austere and rigid ideas, and they were troubled because the spirit of Gandhi was bending and gay. Their teacher proclaimed the sacredness of all life, human and animal, and they were troubled when he ordered that stones be thrown at monkeys who were devouring crops and when he ordered that a calf dying in agony be killed to cut short its suffering. Their teacher also said that robbers and evil men should not suffer outward punishment; they were troubled when he admitted that the world had not yet grown close enough to Truth to practice the ideal completely.

Gandhi could not be rigid toward people; he loved people, and their sufferings and their gropings after Truth moved his heart. He asked them to make not the last step but the next step, and then the next and the next. Thus he found it natural to love those who differed from him and those who did not obey him. He knew that men and women could not reach further than their inward training and experience; hence, despite his hatred of violence, his willingness not to let Hindus make a first step from fear of robbers and fear of Mussalmans and fear of themselves to the higher level of resistance, even if violent; hence his own deep affection for the ancient foundations of Indian life. He wished these foundations to be strengthened so as to carry the great edifice of Truth and non-violence, and he would never stray far from them. For he himself grew step by step. His teaching was ever a progress of spirit, not a code of laws.

But even to the words of Mahatma Gandhi, many men listened according to the habit of men. They did not listen to find out what was said and the spirit in which it was said, putting off judgment until the whole message had come into their minds. Rather they listened in order to set aside, often without knowing it, what they heard in favor of some idea or some fancy that had already made an impress upon them. Some men indeed opened their minds fully. But many understood only in part because they listened only in part.

Yet they loved Gandhi, even when they most differed from him. What could they do? Those who could not agree with him were overwhelmed by him. He would not quarrel with them; rather he would seek to make all truthful compromises. He would chat

92

with them, speaking warmly of the unity he had shared with them in the past and touching upon common ground still shared in the present. He would review the work they had once done side by side. Then he would become quiet and let his adversary argue all his particular ideas. Finally he would speak his own convictions from the reservoir of Truth and experience within him, and he would speak with great sweetness of manner and gentleness of word.

His critics were almost always won over. They were won over so often that certain men, who wished to remain rigid adversaries, refused to talk to Gandhi at all, lest they be carried away from what they thought they believed.

But even when critics were carried away and won over they did not always see that it was Truth that had won them over, and they were greatly perplexed, laying their change of mind to some magnetism peculiar to Gandhi. Thus everyone sensed Truth in Gandhi, but not everyone knew that it was Truth.

If this was the case with Indians, what was the case with Westerners and with those Indians much influenced by the ways of the West? Some heard him and knew what he was. But many, even though they loved him, did not know.

These persons were in some ways like Gandhi's great political heir, Jawaharlal Nehru, a man never outdone in love for Gandhi, a man of great energy, great mind, and great fluency, who made noble sacrifices for freeing his country. He was long the president

93

of the Indian National Congress; Gandhi loved him as a son; the people were moved by him. His father had been leader of the independence party that opposed Gandhi's ideas in the 1920s, and thus his father had been one of Gandhi's close friends. But Nehru was one who had studied and lived much abroad, taking in the ways of the West, and in Nehru the West to some extent looked upon Gandhi as if with its own eyes.

This thoroughly good and sincere man was a constant visitor at Gandhi's ashrams, but he was not a part of them. He was troubled because Gandhi put his mind on the things of the present and let things to come take care of themselves, and he complained that ". . . he refused to look into the future and lay down any long-distance program."

For Gandhi thought first of the spirit of men and very little about the laws by which they would someday be governed. While he was thus looking at present facts, Nehru was looking at future ideas, for looking ahead was what he had learned from the West, which for many centuries has tried to control what cannot be held onto and to blueprint what cannot be put down.

Nehru wished to consider what sort of government there should be so that laws could be passed that would give the people more bread and divide it among them equally, thus insuring the freedom of men's spirit. But Gandhi wished to consider the freedom of men's spirit at once, and let the spirit bring equality of bread. He was little interested in

94

outward government and laws, because he knew that if men seek changes by law instead of by Truth they will not get any changes; if they thus seek equality, they will find inequality; if they thus seek peace, they will find war; and if they thus seek freedom, they will find slavery. Gandhi said, "In matters of conscience the rule of the majority has no place." He was not interested in laws to punish evildoers, for, he said, "All crime is a kind of disease and should be treated as such." Nehru was shocked when Gandhi once told him that Congress should not govern the country but hold aloof in order to act as a non-violent check upon any government the country might develop.

Disagreeing thus with Gandhi, Nehru yet agreed. He said, "Step by step he convinced us of the right-ness of the action, and we went with him, although we did not accept his philosophy. . . . Gandhiji always knew India far better than we did, and a man who could command such tremendous devotion and loyalty must have something that corresponded to the needs and aspirations of the masses." Gandhi indeed sensed in his own heart the needs and the de-sires and the moods and the beliefs of the farmers and artisans of India. He felt their uncertainties as his uncertainties, their changes of emotion as his own changes. He knew also the shifts of emotion of the better off, who were attracted to the old ideas of the West that seemed so new to India. He knew that those who wanted modernity would gather around him at times of forward-going action and that they would go their own way in times of pause. But it was not to them but to the ordinary people that he attuned himself, learning from them the rhythm of struggle and relaxation, understanding when to start a great action and when to cease it, and sensing that there must be pause in outward struggle to give occasion for inward growth.

Therefore, even while Nehru was brooding on his differences with Gandhi, he was deeply moved by him, and he wrote: "What a wonderful man was Gandhiji after all, with his amazing and almost irresistible charm and subtle power over people. His writings and his sayings conveyed little enough impression of the man behind; his personality was far bigger than they would lead one to think. And his services to India, how vast they had been! He had instilled courage and manhood in her people, and discipline and endurance, and the power of joyful sacrifice for a cause, and, with all his humility, pride. Courage is the one sure foundation of character, he had said; without courage there is no morality, no religion, no love. 'One cannot follow truth or love so long as one is subject to fear.' "

Nehru was troubled also that Gandhi's mind was always full of other concerns besides simple independence and the right of Indians to make laws for other Indians. Nehru called them "side issues." But with Gandhi there were no such things as side issues. He said, "I am not interested in freeing India merely from the English yoke. I am bent on freeing India from any yoke whatsoever." When Gandhi undertook his first fast for the untouchables, Nehru was upset, and

96

he wrote, "Would not the larger issues fade into the background? . . ." He feared that Gandhi might die over this smaller issue, and he worried over what then would become of India.

But with Gandhi there were no such things as larger issues. It was as important to nurse the sick at his own ashram as it was to get independence for India, as it was to end untouchability, as it was to live simply, as it was to bring together Hindus and Mussalmans, as it was to spin cotton, as it was to talk joyfully with friends. For there was but one great issue, Truth, and all other issues were in it. The struggle was all the same struggle. If a man could not care for his neighbor and live in peace with him, there would be no power of Truth and non-violence to give India self-rule.

The fast for the untouchables shook Nehru as it shook all India, and Nehru knew that the country could never again be the same, but he did not understand fully how the change had been brought about.

This was the difference between them, and the difference between the way of the West and the way of Gandhi, between the way of the world and the way of Truth, that Nehru looked toward a good government that would make the people right, while Gandhi sought to make the people right and let government take care of itself. He would not have some government legislate equality sometime in the future; he would have men follow it now. Truth is found by freeing men, not by subjecting them to laws that appeal to their selfishness by making them suffer whenever they disobey. Men should suffer willingly for Truth; suffering inflicted upon them for evil is of no use.

What good is it if moneylenders are made to cease oppressing the people if the minds of the moneylenders are not altered? They will still wish to oppress the poor, and this evil is as real as the poverty they wish to cause. Besides, so long as the wish to oppress continues, it will find some manner of expression, and the people will simply be oppressed in a different fashion. This was the essence of Gandhi's teaching: "The slaveowner is more hurt than the slave." "A slave is a slave because he consents to slavery." Nehru complained, "Gandhiji is always thinking in terms of personal salvation and of sin, while most of us have society's welfare uppermost in our minds." But Gandhi knew that Truth acts on the world only as it acts in farmers, workers, barbers, lawyers, housewives, schoolteachers, children, and persons of all sorts. When has Truth acted upon society and not on the men in it?

The difference between these two men was the difference between a practical Gandhi and a less practical Nehru. The world has sought equality by law and got inequality. It has sought peace by force and got war. It has sought good conduct by punishment and got crime. Nehru saw a great chasm between what is practical and what is True, for he was like those men of the world and those men of religion who do not believe in a living God, and thus grant practicality

98

to this world and leave Truth to another. Gandhi was as practical as true religion is practical, but how could Nehru understand religion? He looked at its popular forms and thought it was a thing full of cobwebs and prejudice and old-fashioned fancy. He looked at its deeper aspects and thought it was a matter simply of good ethics. He knew that no one in India had upset ancient evil so greatly as Gandhi, yet he was oppressed because Gandhi had put roots down into ancient faith and in it found Truth.

Nehru was also troubled by what was not essential in Gandhi's teaching (for Truth speaks always through a particular man with a particular man's upbringing, a particular man's nature, and a particular man's needs), and he could not distinguish clearly the pure core of it. He was worried, besides, by Gandhi's inner voice, for he wrote that Gandhi "admitted the presence of this unknown element in him, and said he himself could not answer for it or foretell what it might lead him to do." Such uncertainty oppressed Nehru.

And yet it lifted him up. He wrote of Gandhi that ". . . often the unknown stared at us through his eyes." What the conscious part of Nehru did not agree with, the subconscious part of him yearned to embrace. When Nehru's father died, when Nehru thought of resigning his work as Congress president, or even when he could not decide what to make of Gandhi, he sought Gandhi and found a "wonderfully soothing and healing presence." What is more, he followed him, giving up his own comfort and his own wealth, which was great, reducing his scale of living and even his diet, and at times throwing himself with whole heart into battles even for things about which his mind was not certain. And at all times he loved Gandhi, so that of all the many men who were near him, he perhaps described him best:

"His smile is delightful, his laughter infectious, and he radiates light-heartedness. There is something childlike about him which is full of charm. When he enters a room, he brings a breath of fresh air with him which lightens the atmosphere."

". . . This little man of poor physique had something of steel in him, something rocklike that did not yield to physical powers, however great they might be. And in spite of his unimpressive features, his loincloth and bare body, there was a royalty and a kingliness in him which compelled a willing obeisance from others. Consciously and deliberately meek and humble, yet he was full of power and authority, and he knew it, and at times he was imperious enough, issuing commands which had to be obeyed. His calm, deep eyes would hold one and gently probe into the depths; his voice, clear and limpid, would purr its way into the heart and evoke an emotional response. Whether his audience consisted of one person or a thousand, the charm and magnetism of the man passed on to it, and each one had a feeling of communion with the speaker. This feeling had little to do with the mind, though the appeal to the mind was not wholly ignored. But mind and reason definitely had second place. This process of 'spellbinding' was not brought about by oratory or the hypnotism of silken phrases. The language was always simple and to the point and seldom was an unnecessary word used. It was the utter simplicity of the man and his personality that gripped; he gave the impression of tremendous inner reserves of power."

Gandhi said, "Each one has to find his peace from within. And peace, to be real, must be unaffected by outside circumstances." He said, "God needs no personal service. He serves his creatures without demanding any service for Himself in return. He is unique in this as in many other things. Therefore servants of God are to be known by the service they render to His creatures."

East and West looked at him, followed him, loved him, knew him, and yet misunderstood him.

11

From his simple community
of truth and non-violence
he looked at a world of war.
He led a third struggle against the British,
again was put in jail.

All this time wars in Europe and Asia were stirring beneath the surface of events, and all this time Gandhi was living in his community of peace, the Sevagram Ashram. He would rise at four in the morning, and twenty minutes later he would join in recitations and songs from the scriptures. At five he would take breakfast. He would go out for a brisk walk before the heat of the day grew intense, the while talking to whoever walked with him. At a quarter past six he would go into his mud-and-bamboo hut, which did not have any furniture, and begin writing and talking with those who came to consult him. Before the noon meal he would stop for a half-hour rest. At two he would begin work again, ceasing at five for dinner. From a quarter past six he would work again until evening prayer time. At that time children liked to cuddle around him and look up into his face. He always spent an hour of the day spinning. Formerly he had worked greater hours, for then he had slept no more than four hours night after night.

At his meetings for worship and his meetings for prayer there were no formal invocations or long repetitions. Rather, there was a silence in which all waited and listened. This silence was of such meaning to Gandhi that he observed complete days of it. He said, "It has become both a physical and spiritual necessity for me."

At these meetings there always was singing. There were the chants of the Hindus and the hymns of the Christians. And at regular hours each day a man of Islam would call out the summons to Muhammadan worship. There were also readings from the scriptures. Very often someone read one of Gandhi's favorite verses: "God the ruler pervades all there is in this universe. Therefore renounce and dedicate all to Him, and then enjoy that portion that may fall to thy lot. Never covet anybody's possessions." (Gandhi said of this verse, "This, I say, is my faith and should be the faith of all who call themselves Hindus. And I venture to suggest to my Christian and Mussalman friends that they will find nothing more in their scriptures.")

Gandhi taught that prayer was "a longing of the soul." This prayer was spoken daily: "Lead me from untruth to Truth. Lead me from darkness to light. Lead me from death to immortality."

He would not be rigid in his worship, for he said, "Our whole life is a prayer, and therefore we need not sit down at any particular hour to pray." And he said also, "God knows and anticipates our wants. The Deity does not need my supplication; but I, a

103

very imperfect human being, do need His protection as a child that of his father." Out of prayer rose his experience of Truth, and he said, "Religion is not a thing alien to us; it has to be evolved out of us. It is always within us, with some consciously, with others quite unconsciously. And whether we worship this religious instinct through mental assistance or inward growth, no matter how it is done, it has got to be done if we want to do anything in the right manner or to achieve anything that is going to persist."

At the ashram there were people of all sorts. There was a leper for whom Gandhi cared, as he cared for the other sick, with his own hands. Gandhi said to him, "How can I say 'no' to you? Who will look after you if I don't? I shall build you a hut beside my own, and you will make the place your abode. Even if no one else remains here, you, at least, shall stay."

In the ashram there was also Professor Bhansali, a man of great trouble of spirit, who had sought salvation by living alone in jungles and by closing up his lips with a copper ring. He would not at that time wear any clothes nor would he do any work. Gandhi persuaded him that work for one's fellows is better than life by oneself, and the professor changed his ways: he put on clothes and went into the ashram to labor. But he was still uneasy in mind, and he would seek out his teacher to ask him what he should do and what he should think. Once he came asking permission to hang head down over a well by way of penance. And Gandhi would give over whatever was at hand, abandoning political meetings, conferences with heads of parties, envoys of viceroys, and ambassadors of kings, and talk gently and humorously that his friend's uneasiness might be healed.

There were, in addition, several European and Indian Christians, Hindus of all sorts and origins, a number of Mussalmans, a Japanese Buddhist monk, and a Jew from Poland—a mechanical genius who perfected machines for cottage industries. There were rich and poor, high caste and outcaste, a princess who abandoned a palace, learned men who forswore comfort, doctors and politicians who forgot careers. Gandhi loved to joke gently about the ashram, saying, "I have even likened it to a lunatic asylum—by no means an inappropriate comparison. Surely independence through the spinning wheel can be the proposition only of a lunatic. But luckily lunatics are unaware of their lunacy. And so I regard myself as sane."

From this place of unity and good will, wherein many diverse persons were one family, Gandhi looked upon the outside world. The vision within him of Truth and community was in part made real in the place where he lived, but the world was in great contrast to it.

India first of all was in contrast to it. In 1938 there were fresh outbreaks between Hindus and Mussalmans. The Harijan cause progressed slowly. Gandhi fell into a short period of depression, in the course of which his health suffered, and he said, "I am not likely to live long; maybe I may live a year or a little

105

older. I am going through a process of self-intro-spection, the results of which I cannot foresee. I find myself for the first time during the past fifty years in a slough of despond."

But how could he long remain depressed? In the same year of 1938 he said: "[God] can never be a matter for argument. If you would have me convince others by argument, I am floored. But I can tell you this—that I am surer of His existence than of the fact that you and I are sitting in this room. I can also testify that I may live without air and water but not without Him. You can pluck out my eyes, but that will not kill me. You may chop off my nose, but that will not kill me. But blast my faith in God, and I am dead."

As he sat cross-legged on the floor of his hut at Sevagram he saw not India alone but Europe. He was hurt by what he saw. He recalled that in South Africa no more than 13,000 persons had checked the power of a strong government, and that Indians, by trusting in the power of Truth, had remained in the country although 50,000 Chinese had been driven out. Grieving over the plight of the Jews under Hitler, he said, "If I were a Jew and born in Germany and earned my livelihood there, I would claim Germany as my home, even as the tallest Gentile may, and challenge him to shoot me or to cast me into a dungeon. I would refuse to be expelled or to submit to discriminating treatment."

When he spoke in this way, he was not urging the world to embrace non-violence overnight. He truly

106

believed that Truth would be better advanced if Jews were to flock into concentration camps in a body or stand massed and immobile before their persecutors than it would be if they were to be killed or driven off one by one. There was in Gandhi a sharp and clear sense of the tangible reality of God's strength, and he knew that the only possible next step for all men in all nations was preparation for that reality. Besides, he was convinced of the eventual victory of Truth, even though the new opponent might be a would-be dictator instead of a would-be democrat— greater evil, greater ruthlessness, greater godlessness can be overcome by greater and more determined self-suffering. Gandhi had many times countered varying measures of violence, and he had an experience of non-violence greater than any man else. Out of this experience he said, "Moreover, the non-violent technique does not depend for its success on the good will of the dictator, for a non-violent resister depends upon the unfailing assistance of God, which sustains him throughout difficulties which would otherwise be considered irresistible."

But Gandhi also knew that a people cannot act all at once beyond their training and experience. When he spoke of non-violence and Europe, he spoke of what must happen in time but what could not happen at once. He spoke, as was often his habit, not to utter dictums but to think and feel his way in the world, expressing aloud the varied searchings of his spirit without concern lest he formally contradict himself. He spoke to Europe that he might suggest the uses

107

of Satyagraha and that he might stir people to the first steps of experiment and practice of them.

Thus when Germany cheated her way into Czechoslovakia, he thought again of the power of Truth and of what could happen *if;* he considered that whenever there was the will to resist with Truth, the weapons of Satyagraha could be of better use than the weapons of armies. Fighting availed nothing for Czechoslovakia; not fighting availed nothing either. He denounced the Munich agreement and called it "Peace without Honor."

Gandhi said, "There is no escape from the impending doom save through a bold and unconditional acceptance of the non-violent method. Democracy and violence go ill together. The states that are today nominally democratic will either have to become frankly totalitarian or, if they are to become truly democratic, they must become courageously non-violent."

His experiment was not an experiment of reason but an experiment of faith, and he staked his whole being on it at all-or-nothing odds. He was humble, and he said, "I am by no means sure that I myself am free from self-deception. I have been asked if I may not be mistaken in what I think is God's guidance, and in all Truth I must answer, Yes, very likely."

But the power in him made him cry out in gentle tones that were louder than the rumbling of bombings, ". . . I hear the living Christ saying, these so-called children of mine know not what they are doing. They take my Father's name in vain, for they disobey my Father's central commandment."

108

When war came, Gandhi said, "[Hitler] contemptuously rejected the way of peace and persuasion and chose that of the sword. Hence my sympathy for the cause of the Allies.

"But my sympathy must *not* be interpreted to mean endorsement in any shape or form of the doctrine of the sword for the defense of even proved right. Proved right should be capable of being indicated by right means as against the rude, i.e., sanguinary means."

When war came finally to Europe, it came also to India, for the Viceroy, without consulting any Indian, declared it. A sense of outrage swept the country. The government forbade any talk against war, but this forbidding only made the talk louder. Gandhi was troubled because the people were still treated as vassals of Empire; and the members of Congress, to which Gandhi no longer belonged, were even more troubled. The war laws were challenged nonviolently all over the country and many thousands went into jail. At the ashram, Professor Bhansali undertook and completed a sixty-day fast.

Before long the war in Asia spread, and the Japanese pushed across the country of Burma and came close to India. At that time the British sent Sir Stafford Cripps with proposals for the postwar dominion status of the country and for immediately increased Indian government of the land. But the British insisted that they retain all measures of defense, and in wartime the powers of defense can be all powers.

Gandhi himself shrank from the thought of an India fighting violently in war. But he was ready even to let his own views on the power of Truth be overridden by Congress were India to be put truly into the hands of the Indians. But Congress, on the one hand, would not believe that the British were sincere in their promise of postwar freedom, even though Gandhi, despite many decades of seeing promises broken, was convinced that the British should be trusted. And the British, on the other hand, would give Indians no part in the direction of their country's defense.

Gandhi would not, therefore, attempt to dissuade Congress from rejecting the British proposals. The British were then driving farmers out of their homes, without notice or compensation, to make space for airports and other military places, and Gandhi considered that however much good faith there might be in offering more self-government, there would not be more self-government, and that government would be swallowed up by the rule of the British military and there would not be any change.

He watched the war, seeing in it the forging of another link in the continuing circle of violence. For he saw not only the conflict at hand, but conflicts past and conflicts to come. There is a passage in the Hindu scriptures which reads, "First there comes the wagging of tails, then the bark, then the replying bark, then the turning of·one round the other, then the showing of teeth, then the roaring, and then comes

110

the commencement of the fight. It is the same with men; there is no difference whatsoever."

What he had said long before he had believed deeply ever since: "Brute force has been ruling the world for thousands of years, and mankind has been reaping its bitter harvest all along, as he who runs may read. There is little hope of anything good coming out of it in the future. Therefore, if light can come out of darkness, then alone can love emerge from hatred."

Hence he said to the world, "Fight Nazism without anger and with non-violent arms. I would like you to lay down the arms that you have as being useless for saving you or humanity.

"I hold a new order to be impossible if the war is fought to a finish or if mutual exhaustion leads to a patched-up peace.

"My notion of democracy is that under it the weakest should have the same opportunity as the strongest. That can never happen except through non-violence. No country in the world today shows any but patronizing regard for the weak."

He knew, of course, that Europe and America would not then fight without violence. But he believed that India could, and he proposed that the country offer Satyagraha against the oncoming Japanese. He was deeply mindful of the cost, and he said that he would be willing to sacrifice half the lives of the people of India in battling the Japanese with the power of Truth.

But this could not be, and Britain continued to

run India as a conquered land. Indians became wrathful. Gandhi remained gentle, but he said, "I do not wish to humiliate the British. But the British must go. I am more than ever convinced that Britain cannot win this war unless she leaves India." When he spoke in this way, he spoke of the moral loss that brings physical loss.

Knowing that the British would not abandon violence for non-violence, he did not insist on such a change as a condition for their forces remaining in India; he would not stand in the way. He did not even know whether an Indian government might not become war-mad, once freedom had been won. But he did know that India needed at once to become free that she might be weaned away from her own weakness and her distrust for her rulers, and that Britain needed India's freedom that she might regenerate her own self.

On May 8, 1942, there began all over India a third great battle of non-violence, a quit-India campaign addressed to the rule of the British. Britons and Americans read part of what Gandhi had said and many of them put him down angrily as a self-seeking politician and possibly a traitor. A few months later, the government put him in jail.

But it was thus that this great soul had appealed to the British: ". . . I do claim to be a passionate searcher after Truth, which is but another name for God. In the course of that search the discovery of non-violence came to me. To spread it is my life's work. I have no interest in living except for the prosecution of that mission. May God give power to every word of mine. In His name I began to write this, and in His name I end it."

During this period he studied much the ways of the world, but he studied the ways of Truth still more. Thus he said, "Truth is like a vast tree which yields more and more fruit the more you nourish it." He said also, "All sins are committed in secrecy. The moment we realize that God witnesses even our thoughts we shall be free." He knew from his own experience of it that there was nothing more constant, nothing more real, nothing more compelling, and nothing more powerful than freedom, which is Truth, and Truth, which is God. Throughout the long years of war he increasingly set this Truth over against violence.

12

*India became free. But the country,
freed by a man of non-violence,
fell into violence, and the man
of the power of Truth
died from the power of a bullet.*

Finally there came an end to the forging of the second link of the chain of great wars, and with it came hope that Gandhi's battle for freedom, begun forty years earlier in South Africa, might come to partial victory. It was not a complete victory, and it would not bring the yoke-free India that Gandhi yearned for. But he would not stand in the way of it.

He had wanted a land ruled by Truth and non-violence, and what was given was a land ruled, as other lands were ruled, by ceremony and armies. He had wanted a land in which the farmers could take over the farms by non-violent refusal to pay rents to landlords, and in which the poor could win equality by declining to fit in with the wealth-getting of the rich. And what was given was a land of outward law and order. He had wanted a land of which 700,000 villages would be the centers of government, and what was given was a government centered in one place. He had wanted above all else a country healed of its wounds of prejudice, and what was given was a country split into two parts, Hindu and Mussal-man. Yet he knew the facts of growth, and he would not, out of regret that India was not able to take greater steps, prevent her from taking one single great step toward freedom.

Therefore, while other men called in question the sincerity of the British decision to grant the freedom India had herself won, Gandhi put his trust in it, arguing with the politicians, explaining to the crowds, writing for the papers. Throughout long talks and wrangles he quietly sought the best ways for the transfer of power from government to government. And in this he won total victory, for after the British rule was ended, hatred and distrust of Britain vanished from India and the power of Truth was victorious, even as Gandhi had said that it would be victorious, without bitterness.

At one minute past midnight on August 15, 1947, in the city of Delhi, the new government was instituted with ceremony and display, and the politicians of India scrambled for position and honor. But Gandhi was not there. He had put himself into a third-class carriage and had started off to the village of Noakhali, where he planned at the age of seventy-eight to walk from house to house that he might serve the people. His spirit was fresh, and he said that if it were God's will he would live to the age of one hundred and twenty-five.

Suddenly the searing drama of Truth pitted against evil flared up toward a terrible end. The India freed

115

by the man who put his faith in the power of Truth and eschewed violence erupted in violent passion. In the villages there was relative quiet, but in the cities and towns Hindu beset Mussalman and Mussalman beset Hindu in vast waves of looting and slaughter so that tens of thousands were killed and millions forced out of their homes.

For it was thus that the world, bested by Truth, struck back at it. The people who had brought their babies that Gandhi's hand might rest on their heads, the people who had waited in great lines that they might simply let their eyes rest on him, the people who, according to their means, had put up marble busts or hung photographs or treasured post cards of him, the people who worshiped him—these people had heard him without understanding him enough.

The orthodox of one religion drew together against the orthodox of another. Politicians connived. Revolutionists erupted and helped pit group against group. Afraid of the wrath of the people, afraid of the opinion of the world, India's new political leaders, all of them Gandhi's old co-workers, knew not what to say, and they said little. The old lieutenant Sardar Patel even gave Hindu extremists nods of encouragement. It was Nehru, who had the greatest outward differences of opinion, who had the greatest inward feeling of closeness to Gandhi, but even he had not understood Truth deeply enough to argue it.

A great sadness of spirit came upon Gandhi. Depression had not been upon him since the riots of 1938. He had long foreseen the danger of country-

116

wide bloodshed and he had long worked to keep it away. Twenty years earlier he had said, "A government can give protection against thieves and robbers, but not even an independent government will be able to protect against a wholesale boycott by one community or another. . . . Hindus and Mussalmans, if they desire independence, have perforce to settle their differences amicably." And Gandhi had also expected confusion at the end of the rule of the British. He had even urged that India be left to God or to anarchy, for he felt that in the climate of freedom the evils of the country would to some degree work themselves out. But the eruption of India and the sudden casting up of the wickedness of centuries overwhelmed him.

Some of his oldest friends had died, but their deaths had not cast him down, for he felt warmth and love rather than grief. Maganlal Gandhi, a relative and closest of his followers, had died in 1928. Vithalbhai Patel, one of his most able political followers, had died in 1933. C. F. Andrews, his great British friend, who had met him first in South Africa, who had sat beside him during fasts, and who had saved his life in 1934, had died in 1940. Rabindranath Tagore, whose poetry had brought light into Gandhi's spirit, had died in 1941. Mahadev Desai, his friend, secretary, and Boswell, had died at his side in prison in 1942. His wife Kasturbai, who had followed him devotedly for sixty-two years, taking the changes and the hardships of his life along with him, had died in prison in 1944. But the changes of death did not sorrow Gandhi's spirit.

117

And as for his own death, he was so far from fearing it that he was ready to welcome it whenever it might come. He once said, "Our scriptures tell us that childhood, old age, and death are incidents only to this perishable body of ours, and that man's spirit is eternal and immortal. That being so, why should we fear death? And where there is no fear of death there can be no sorrow over it either."

Gandhi had also seen the course of a terrifying world war wherein there had been let loose weapons of wholesale annihilation, and he had seen the aftermath of it, which gave little promise of peace. He had seen darkness and madness in the world. But he had felt light in India. He was not distressed at the thought that the physical world might sometime dissolve through the agency of some such thing as the atom bomb. For the present, he believed that non-violence and simplicity were the true defenses against annihilation, for of what use is it to drop expensive bombs on inexpensive cities? Besides, he had also grown in the truth that evil lies not in being killed but in killing. His great faith was that the light kindled in India would give light to the world.

When the light flickered, his spirit was shaken. He looked at the violence of India and he said, "There is no place for me. I have given up hope of living for one hundred and twenty-five years. I might last a year or two, but that is a different matter." On his seventy-eighth birthday he said, "Why do I receive all these congratulations? . . . The time was when whatever I said, the masses followed. But today I am a lone voice in India." And he prophesied sadly, "The fear haunts me that India must yet go through a deeper blood bath." When visitors asked him about his teaching of non-violence, he recalled an experience in South Africa when someone had introduced him as the leader of the weak and he had risen to protest that he was the leader of the strong, who alone are capable of non-violence. And he said that if he had known then what he knew now he would not have called himself a leader of the strong.

But when he was asked whether he was not being overmuch pessimistic, he answered that he was not pessimistic at all, that he believed in Truth and would hold to it although the whole world was set against him. His suffering was not a suffering that lost him any faith in Truth and its power; it was a suffering that laid burdens of responsibility upon him, for he took the evil of the land as his own evil. Therefore he sought the way by which he could heal India and purify himself.

His voice and his whole being talked tirelessly, pleading and arguing and reproaching. But his words did not by themselves arrest the bloodshed. Then a voice spoke in him and he went to H. S. Suhrawardy, once Moslem Premier of the province of Bengal and a man much hated by Hindus, and proposed that the two of them should live in one house in the bloodiest section of bloody Calcutta. And when the two men had gone into the house, there came a great crying out from Hindus, saying that Gandhi was betraying them. But of a sudden quiet came upon the city. After

119

a while violence returned briefly, and Gandhi began a fast of purification. After seventy-three hours the city rallied around him, and quiet came again and was unbroken. But a little while later the Hindus and their cousins the Sikhs took steps to drive the Mussalmans out of the city of Delhi, and Gandhi went there to take residence in the house of an industrialist named Birla, a man whose person he loved but whose mills he hated.

All the while he pleaded not simply for an end of bloodshed but for a coming together of the two severed parts of the country. He went out into crowds and talked endlessly with leaders and people that there might be unity. At the end of his meetings of prayer he was sustained by the closing words, *Shanti, Shanti, Shanti*—peace, peace, peace.

Into the city of Delhi there came peace, but peace did not come into the outlying parts of it, and again Gandhi fasted. This fast stirred the people greatly.

But it did not stir all of the people. On the third day of it a crowd of Hindus came shouting, "Let Gandhi die." Nehru, who had become Prime Minister of the Hindu part of India, was then coming into the house where Gandhi lay, and this man of heart and intellect was moved to non-violent protest without even thinking of it, and he dashed impulsively after the crowd, calling out, "How dare you say that? Kill me first! Kill me first!"

Some days later a bomb was set off outside the wall of the house. But Gandhi would not allow any precautions. Once Communists had tried to do injury to him,

120

and that same evening he said to half a million people, "I keep no bodyguard to protect me. My chest is literally bare." Another time a bomb was thrown against his car, and he announced that he would travel by ox-cart instead of by car so as not to place obstacles between himself and assassins. Therefore, when friends came asking permission to search for arms all people who came about the Birla house, he refused it.

The dissatisfaction in Delhi was the dissatisfaction of a few. During the fast quiet came again upon the place and the Hindu and Mussalman leaders hurriedly came together to pledge a peace that would not be broken. Then Gandhi stopped his fast and took nourishment, and he made ready to go on with his battle.

Eleven days later he said, as he had said many times in the past, a verse of his native area of Gujarat:

> *This is a strange world.*
> *How long have I to play this game?*

The next afternoon he spoke for some time with Sardar Patel, who stood so firmly against the Mussalman part of India that he even counseled war. Gandhi said of him that he had thorns in his tongue, and Gandhi talked to him sweetly and persuasively. Then he looked at the dollar watch that hung from his loincloth and excused himself to go outside to his regular prayer meeting.

He went forth with his hands upon the shoulders of Ava and Manu, his grandnieces, and they supported him as he walked up three steps to a platform.

Then a short, thick young man named Godse, a young intellectual who had been sitting near the platform, came to Gandhi and knelt at his feet, saying, "You are late today for the prayer."

Gandhi said, "Yes, I am."

The young man brought out a pistol and shot three times. Gandhi's hands came together in the gesture of greeting, and as he fell he said softly, "Ai Rama, Ai Rama—O God, O God."

Half an hour later one of the disciples came out of the house and said to the multitude sorrowing outside, "Bapuji [father] is finished."

To the pyre on which the body of the Great Soul was burned Nehru came, and he wept and said, "Bapuji, here are flowers. Today, at least, I can offer them to your bones and ashes. Where will I offer them tomorrow, and to whom?"

Thus the world finally confronted Gandhi and did violence upon him. The man of the power of Truth died from the power of a bullet. Thus also did Truth confront the world and win victory over it. In this was the victory: that the world which could still Gandhi's voice could not still his great soul, the living witness to that for which men hunger, the conquest of evil by good. Whether the victory be of this time or some later time, the overwhelming flood of Truth released by the self-suffering of good men is again upon the world. Whether men or nations live or die, each man and all men are regirded with a power greater than weapons, greater than governments, greater than wealth, fame, or success, greater than any of the devices by which men attempt to hide from God.

COMMENT

This account of Gandhi is an attempt not to evaluate him but to show him and his impact upon his world. The writer has tried to stand as little in the way as possible. Inevitably, however, he does stand somewhat in the way, and he must explain and excuse what he has shown and what he has not. There is omitted, for instance, a recounting of such matters as Gandhi's distaste for food and sex and his fondness for cow worship. The writer justifies these omissions on grounds of inward certainty that Gandhi's teaching on such subjects is not germane to the condition of Western men and women, and he begs excuse in Gandhi's own words:

"We shall err, and sometimes grievously in our application. But man is a self-governing being, and self-government necessarily includes the power as much to commit errors as to set them right as often as they are made."

On other matters of judgment the writer has tried so far as possible to let Gandhi's life carry the argument. No solution has been attempted to the question whether or not Gandhi compromised too much with

124

the mood of the people of India, whether he culti-
vated old roots too carefully to grow enough strong
new fruit. No case is made as to whether Gandhi is a
freak of circumstance or a man of genuine power of
Truth. No reasoning is put forward as to whether
there is in fact a living Deity who is Truth and whose
universe responds to non-violence. On such questions
there can be no outward certainty; there can be only
faith or doubt arising from the impact of a life of
overwhelming inward richness and outward multi-
plicity, confronted with which intellectual argument
becomes sterile. In the face of Gandhi's Truth, the
writer, an incomplete person, can only state his faith
and his desire to grow in it.

This book, a very reduced extract of a very broad
life, springs in part from other books, and it is sug-
gested that it be used as a springboard back to them.
The great source works on Gandhi are his own writings, not yet collected into any set of complete works
but scattered among many and valuable sources. The
main Gandhi writings in English are *The Story of My
Experiments with Truth, Satyagraha in South Africa,
Hind Swaraj,* and, in particular, the magazines *Young
India* and *Harijan.* Articles from *Young India* have
been collected in the form of several books, much to
be recommended because they show the complex and
continuing unrolling of a single and harmonious spirit.
The writer is particularly indebted to *Young India,
1924-1926,* published by the Viking Press in 1927.
Similar collections of *Harijan* articles are not

available, but there are books in which separate articles from that magazine appear along with other valuable material. Of these, the writer has found the following helpful: *My Appeal to the British,* by Mahatma Gandhi, John Day, 1942, a sympathetic collection of Gandhi's ideas about World War II; *What Does Gandhi Want?* by T. A. Ramand, Oxford University Press, 1942, a less sympathetic treatment of the same subject; *Satyagraha in Gandhiji's Own Words,* All India Congress Committee, 1935; *Teachings of Mahatma Gandhi,* edited by Jag Parvesh Chander. *A Week with Gandhi,* by Louis Fischer, Duell, Sloan & Pearce, 1942, gives a clear picture of Gandhi at work. Muriel Lester's *My Host the Hindu* and *Entertaining Gandhi,* published in Britain in 1931 and 1932, give absorbing detail of one period of his life.

Among general biographies that draw heavily on Gandhi's own writing, special attention should be called to Romain Rolland's study, *Mahatma Gandhi,* 1924, and to the three great volumes by Gandhi's close friend, C. F. Andrews: *Mahatma Gandhi's Ideas, Mahatma Gandhi, His Own Story,* and *Mahatma Gandhi at Work,* published in the United States in 1930 and 1931 by Macmillan. These three books cover Gandhi's life and teaching up to the stirrings of the Civil Disobedience campaign in 1928. They are well supplemented by two books of Krishnalal Shridharani, *The Mahatma and the World,* Duell, Sloan & Pearce, 1946, and particularly *War without Violence,* an intensive study of the principles and practices of

Satyagraha, published in 1939 by Harcourt Brace & Co. The writer has found help from *Mahatma Gandhi, His Life, Work, and Influence,* by Jashwant Rao Chitambar, the John C. Winston Co., 1933; from *Sword of Gold,* by Roy Walker, published by Indian Independence Union in Britain in 1945; and from *Mahatma Gandhi, Essays and Reflections on His Life and Work,* a collection of appraisals of Gandhi edited by S. Radhakrishnan and published by G. Allen & Unwin, Ltd., 1939. Finally there is rich material in Jawaharlal Nehru's autobiography, published in the United States by the John Day Company in 1941 under the title *Toward Freedom.* Nehru's general writings on Gandhi have been brought together in a book published in 1948 by John Day under the title *Nehru on Gandhi.* There are numerous other books of value; the present list is by no means inclusive.

To all of these books, to *Time* magazine, February 9, 1948, and to the article of William Stuart Nelson, *The Gandhi I Knew,* in the *Friends Intelligencer,* May 15, 1948, the writer is indebted.

The writer wishes to express thanks to the John Day Company for permission to quote from *Towards Freedom,* and to the Macmillan Company, publishers of C. F. Andrews's works.

The writer wishes also to express warm personal thanks to Albert L. Furth, Hermann Hagedorn, John Haynes Holmes, Helen S. Maurer, A. J. Muste, William S. Schlamm, and J. J. Singh, whose comments have been of great value. Responsibility for the material and its presentation rests, of course, with the writer.

The reader's attention is called to the fact that punctuation, capitalization, and paragraphing, which are not uniform in Gandhi's articles as originally published, have been standardized. On page 47 liberty has been taken to translate *ahimsa* as non-violence, on page 48 *chapatti* as bread without yeast, and on page 105 *swaraj* as independence.